Charlie,
Mom knows that
some day you
will catch the
Big One

12/25/81

HOW THE EXPERTS CATCH TROPHY FISH

By the same Author

America's Best Bay, Surf, and Shoreline Fishing
America's Best Lake, Stream, and River Fishing
America's Best Deep-Sea Fishing
Catching Freshwater Fish Made Easy

HOW THE EXPERTS CATCH TROPHY FISH

Heinz Ulrich

South Brunswick and New York:
A. S. Barnes and Company
London: Thomas Yoseloff Ltd

Library of Congress Catalogue Card Number: 68-27237

A. S. Barnes and Co., Inc.
Cranbury, New Jersey

Thomas Yoseloff Ltd
108 New Bond Street
London W. 1, England

SBN 498-06586-3
Printed in the United States of America

ACKNOWLEDGMENTS

I should like to personally thank each of the excellent anglers in this book for giving their time and so generously sharing their vast fishing knowledge.

CONTENTS

HOW THE EXPERTS CATCH TROPHY FISH

FRESHWATER FISHING

1. ATLANTIC SALMON FISHING WITH DON LEYDEN

The Atlantic salmon is a majestic fish that spends most of its adult life in the ocean only coming into cold clear freshwater streams to breed. These fish require the coldest clearest water, rich in oxygen to survive their spawning runs. Salmon were once plentiful in many of our Northeastern streams, but because of polution that fish is now practically extinct in most United States waters. Still, this does not stop American anglers from becoming salmon enthusiasts for a regular small army of fishermen annually make their way up to New Brunswick and other North East Canadian Providences for the superb sport of Atlantic salmon fishing.

Donald Leyden, who is the manager of the New York office of the Hampden Glazed Paper and Card Company, is an ardent Atlantic salmon angler. He regularly takes the 800 mile trip to his favorite fishing stream, the Miramichi in New Brunswick. To him these salmon are the biggest and finest fish that can be taken by fly fishing and there just isn't any other sport to compare to this fishing.

Atlantic salmon anglers will tell you they are intrigued by the fact that with a few bits of feathers on a hook the angler will lure 3 to 30 pound fish. These fish must be induced to rise from a depth of 4 to 10 feet to hit a fly they have no business going after. The long history of this sport that comes down to us from the European noblemen and kings who fly fished the streams of England and Scotland for salmon adds additional luster.

Donald Leyden started his salmon fishing back in 1950 and by his own admission actually had no business going at it in the first place. He had been tying his own trout flies, but as he studied fly patterns, he saw the most beautiful flies were the salmon flies which he was tying and giving away. Then he began reading about salmon and there grew an urge to fish his flies to see if they would really take these fish. Soon thereafter he took his first trip to the Miramichi where the salmon really took him, for every year thereafter he has visited the stream. Lately, together with several of his fishing buddies, he purchased his own fishing water on the river at the site of one of his favorite fishing pools.

The Miramichi, according to many anglers, including Mr. Leyden, is the finest almon stream on the North American continent. This stream gets more salmon in it than any other stream in North America for it is a perfect breeding stream as it has cold clear water and a gravel bottom along its whole distance. The regulars of this stream do admit that it does not hold the biggest salmon in the world; 30 pounds is generally considered to be top weight here. Some North American streams get a few bigger fish and European waters on occasion have had fish more than twice this size, but the Miramichi anglers insist that mile for mile no stream will hold more fish than their's.

Fishing on the Miramichi begins in the middle of May immediately after ice out. The fish in the river at this time are the ones that had spawned in the fall of the previous year and have spent a winter under the ice living off their own fat. These fish are referred to as black salmon or slinks, and they are considerably different from the sea fresh salmon that will come upstream a short while later. The slinks are a dark color and are thin with practically no belly on them. Even the methods of fishing them are far different, for this fishing lacks all the finesse of the summer and fall sport. These black salmon are anxious to get back to the sea and they get carried downstream in the current behind the broken ice. During the spring these fish are starved and they take virtually anything thrown in front of them. They are generally fished with large streamer flys measuring 3 to 6 inches in length. Anglers fish from anchored canoes and they let their fly out behind the boat and strip the fly line in again. This action is repeated again and again until a fish hits. Don Leyden readily points out that he never took part in spring salmon fishing, and more emphatically insists he never will.

Directly behind a shad run, about June 15th, the first bright salmon from the ocean will enter the stream. These early salmon of late June and July are beautiful fish. They are a pure silvery color with spotted back and dark fins. They head upstream slowly, traveling mostly at night and resting in the salmon holes during the days. Their goal is the headwaters of the river some 200 miles away, but they have until fall to get there. These first fish are considered exceptional prizes for they are most explosive on a hook and are the hardest to catch. Then these salmon are far fewer in number than the accumulation of fish that enter the river later on, and should the angler be so lucky and skillful to hook one, he has an added problem for the fish have tissue paper mouths. Hooks rip from them so easily that even the best anglers have difficulty holding one and the slightest error in fighting technique means a lost fish. Don Leyden has caught his fair share of these early fish and he feels that in spite of the extra difficulty in taking them, their fight and beauty more than make up for these problems.

More fish will continue coming into the river throughout July, depending upon the water level of the stream. If the water level is high the schools of fish come in, but when the water level is very low the fish stay out in the estuaries. Generally, the main run of Atlantic salmon begins in the middle of August and continues on through September and October. These are the fish that spread themselves out over the whole length of the stream, and these are the fish that will be the major target of the army of salmon anglers. Don Leyden always makes it a point to be on the stream in September—generally about the middle of September—for this will be when most fish are in the stream. Also, the commercial netters' season closes at September 1st, and when their gill nets are out of the mouth of the river and the nearby estuaries, it allows the fish free access to the stream.

Fall begins the breeding season for the salmon and many of the late entering fish never make it to the headwaters. The Miramichi has a gravel bottom along its entire 200 miles of main stream as well as in its 200 or more miles of tributaries. This is what makes this such an excellent salmon stream, for here the ripe female can always find a quiet gravel bed to construct her nest and deposit her eggs. There are usually males close by, so few eggs are wasted. After spawning, the Atlantic salmon will continue to live in the river until the following spring when they will make their way downstream and back to the ocean. Unlike the Pacific salmon which spawn once and die the Atlantic salmon may spawn two and even three times.

The newborn salmon are referred to as Parr, and these fish will live in the river. Salmon remain a stream fish for 3½ to 4½ years, during which time they are called a smolts, and during these years they live much like trout, feeding on insects and other usual trout food. It is throughout this life that they develop the instinct to strike at an insect, an instinct that they never lose. At the end of their smolt period they enter the sea where they feed, grow rapidly, then 1 or 2 years later return in schools weighing 3 to 5 pounds each. Other fish remain at sea 2 or 3 years and they may return weighing 8 to 10 pounds, while those that remain out for 4 years might weigh 15 pounds on their first spawning run. It is generally agreed that the biggest of the salmon taken are the fish that return for their second or third spawning run.

Don Leyden says, "You're doing good fishing if you take one Atlantic salmon a day." There are, of course, days when an angler may approach the legal limit of 4 fish, and there may be streaks when an angler may get his 20-fish limit in a week. Persons unfamiliar with salmon fishing would be suprised to know that released fish count towards the limit of 4 a day. Mr. Leyden and every other salmon angler knows that these are extremely difficult fish to take as they are protected by law and may only be taken fly fishing. None of these anglers however, would have it any other way. It is extremely hard to get a salmon to take a fly, and then because they are so big and strong they are very difficult to land, all in all making them one of the most elusive and finest sportfish that swims. One of Don's friends sums up Atlantic salmon fishing by saying: "It is like playing poker for high stakes."

When the salmon move upstream they usually move at night, stopping to rest in the salmon pools during the days. Actually a salmon pool is not a pool in the trout sense of the word at all, but it will merely be any stretch of water where the fish regularly rest. Many of the pools are regular stretches of water where there are a few small rocks strewn over a gravel bottom. A salmon will come up behind a rock, put its nose right up to this rock (which may be the size of a softball), and rest much of the day in that position. A few yards away another fish may be resting, and a little further away another one—thus that area is a salmon pool. The anglers will see fish behind these same rocks day after day, yet they know they are not the same fish, for the migrating salmon move upstream, only stopping to rest. What happens is the fish coming in behind go to the exact spots that the fish before them have evacuated. Salmon continue going to these spots day after day, and even year after year, providing that changing water conditions or ice will not disrupt the contour of the bottom. Many people on the Miramichi have tried to create artificial salmon holes by strewing rocks over the bottom. Some of these have worked very well, but like all salmon pools, they are subject to change. Don points out that the winter ice and excessive high water will change some of the pools so radically that they may completely disappear, while other stretches that were dead water will become new pools.

There are four types of water on the Miramichi, and Don

Leyden points out that these four types are basic to all salmon fishing. A salmon angler must be able to recognize each one in order to determine just how good the fishing will be in that immediate section of river. The first type of water important to the anglers is fast water that has a broken rippling surface with some rapids and patches of whiteness on its surface. This will hold the small salmon, but it seldom has the large fish. This first water will often be referred to as "Duffer water" because it is water in which an angler will not have to be too careful about the drift of his fly. Here the broken surface and the fast moving current very nicely cover mistakes of fly presentation.

The second type of water is slower moving, but still has a rippling surface and a brisk moving current. The most important thing in this kind of water is that it has a broken bottom where the fish can stop to rest. These are the stretches where rocks strewn about to create artificial pools will generally perform best. This type of water holds the most salmon and it is the kind of salmon pool to which Don Leyden would take a neophyte angler. Here will be the biggest concentrations of all sized fish, and this kind of salmon pool offers everyone a good chance for a fish. Experts and beginners alike will find the medium-fast broken bottom water is the best spot to pick up those fine salmon in the 7 to 12 pound class.

Where the stream widens out and the water moves more slowly is the third kind of water to look for. Here the stream will generally be deeper and at times may appear as if the surface is not moving. However, this type of water must have movement if it is to be good for salmon since these fish need the current. Sometimes the major movement of the stream will be below the surface, but to qualify as a salmon pool it must have current to supply the fish the oxygen they need. Salmon may often be seen resting in this kind of pool with their gills opening and closing to absorb oxygen. Stretches of this type are the expert pools, for they will hold those fish that exceed 20 pounds. The expert pools are challenging to the fisherman since they have slower surface water making fly presentation more difficult and then the deep water makes it more difficult to raise a fish. It requires extreme skill to fish an expert pool, nevertheless many of the anglers spend much of their time here in quest for the biggest fish.

A fourth kind of water is a large pool where there is hardly any movement either on the surface or below it. Salmon anglers refer to this as a "stink hole," because it is dead water that seldom, if ever, contains fish. One of the dangers of spooking fish from good water is that they move back into a stink hole where no one can get them. All anglers avoid fishing the obvious dead sections.

The most important point of salmon fishing comes after the angler is on the stream and has selected his water for fishing. Now he must present a fly in such a manner that it interests the salmon. Don Leyden feels the main point is to get the fly right over the nose of the fish so that he can see it and get interested in it. He feels far too many anglers stress great casting distance as being most important in this fishing, however this is all wrong. He says, "I can control my casts up to about 70 feet, but most of my fish are taken with casts of 40 feet or less. Other anglers will find their best catches generally come within this radius too." He points out that these are monstrous fish who after a life in the ocean have a sureness about themselves. They do not act like ordinary nervous stream fish, and to illustrate this point, Don has often waded so close to the fish that he actually poked them on the sides with his rod tip. Even then the fish merely moved several feet away, more annoyed than scared. Salmon can of course be spooked, and most of the time it happens by the man who does excessive wading in the middle of the stream. Since salmon need the current they are basically midstream fish, hence an anglers best fishing is done somewhat from the shore by throwing the fly out towards center stream.

A downstream cast angled out at about 45 degrees from the shore is the standard cast used by most salmon fishermen. It is generally thought that this is the best cast since it gives a fly its best drift which is extremely important in fly presentation. This cast will give the fly a good sweep of the water where it first floats downstream, and then sweeps in towards shore in a gentle arch. The fly will at all times be looking as if it were an insect floating in the water. Should there be an eddy, or should the fly get in the backwater of a rock and lose its natural motion, the angler quickly lifts up and casts again, or he mends his line to correct the fault.

On many occasions there will be fish in positions that cannot be fished to by the usual downstream cast. Then the angler has to cast out, and by mending his line must keep the big bow, that the current makes, out of the line. When a bow occurs, the fly will follow it getting whipped through the water much faster than a natural float, thus being unnatural looking and unproductive. Generally the longer and the more cross current an angler casts the bigger and quicker a bow develops. Mr. Leyden feels an angler is always better off when trying to work in closer to the fish where he has a better chance for a correct presentation of the fly.

Many items are important in whether a salmon takes a fly or merely lets it pass over its head possibly 100 to 200 times without ever budging. Light is one of these very important points. To illustrate this Don Leyden explains that there are only certain times during bright sunny day when the salmon will be prone to take a fly, viz, in the mornings from sunrise until about 10 A.M., and then again from about 3:30 P.M. until dusk. One tip this top angler gives his fellow sportsmen is that "Most anglers quit fishing by 4:30 P.M., but I've taken more salmon after that time than at any other time during the day."

Few fish are ever taken during the middle of the day because the sun is shining overhead and down on the water. At this time the fish hardly ever see a fly for it is lost in the brightness above them. The same holds true during other times of the day whenever the sun is in front of the fish and is shining brightly onto the water so that a fish cannot see a fly presented to it. Although silhouette flies have been developed to help anglers on bright days, the perfect light is still when the sun is low on the horizon, behind the fish and making no glare. This gives the fish a clear unobstructed view of everything in front of him. A cloudy day also aids a fish's visibility of the surface and flies.

Mr. Leyden goes on to explain that the best Atlantic salmon anglers are scientific fishermen. He feels that a good fly presentation is the one that interests the fish enough to strike; therefore, each condition of when a fish takes a fly, how the fly was presented, the size and type of fly used, and the angle of the fly in relation to the fish should be recalled. Good anglers will then try to approach another salmon in exactly the same way they had successfully approached a fish under similar circumstances. The angler who learns to duplicate his own or others successful actions will soon find that his fish catch will increase. Where this is especially important in Atlantic salmon fishing, it is just as true for other fishing too.

Sometimes an angler will have his fly float downstream and suddenly a big splash will indicate a salmon has struck. If the fish is missed the angler's natural tendency will be to cast directly back to that spot. Don Leyden says this is wrong for that angler will be fishing behind the fish. Instead the angler should make exactly the same cast he had made before for the salmon will have followed the fly on the first cast. After striking, that salmon will immediately return to his same spot in the river. Thus the angler, by repeating his first cast, gets another sweep over the fish's head. Don Leyden suggests taking three or four more casts to that spot and then changing flies and taking some more casts right there in a continuing effort to raise that fish again.

A salmon comes up at a fly differently from the way other fish rise. This fish may on occasions come up from a depth of 10 feet to hit at a fly, although most of the fish will be taken where the water is 4 to 6 feet deep. The salmon's rise is a slow and exact head-to-tail movement up at the fly which it takes very deliberately.

Most salmon anglers will have had previous trout fishing experience, therefore they have a tendency to strike their line as the fish hits the fly. This, Don Leyden feels, is not the best way to fish for it is best to let the salmon have the fly as he will hook himself. By striking the line the angler too often snaps the fly away from these slow rising fish. Some of the salmon anglers will violently disagree with fisherman Leyden's method of hooking salmon because they advocate striking on a hit. These anglers will generally admit to missing some fish by striking, but they will insist it is worth a few misses to know that the fish you do hook is on solidly. This doesn't add up to Don Leyden, for he maintains that any salmon that does take the fly will hook himself solidly enough, and with a greater percentage of hookups by waiting, it is to the angler's advantage to hold back on striking a line.

Once the fish is hooked and the fight starts in earnest, the angler will really see the beauty of Atlantic salmon, for they literally explode. These are fish strong enough to work upstream against frightening rapids and falls (they regularly jump 6 foot waterwalls) and they now turn all this power against the line. Don Leyden warns that the first thing an angler must learn to do is to control the fight so that the fisherman and not the fish is in charge. Too many anglers simply let the salmon be in control and they lose many fish this way. He says, "Most people don't play a fish they let the fish play them."

Mr. Leyden points out that most anglers are shy about getting a big bend in their rods, and consequently they let the fish take control. At one time, Don Leyden tested the medium action fly rod, which he now uses regularly, to see just how many pounds of pressure would be exerted at hook level when he gets a good round bend in his rod. He was amazed when the scale showed that he was exerting less than three pounds of pressure on the payload of the line. This clearly showed him why it was so important to keep pressure on his hooked fish, for even with a full bent rod the angler is exerting less pressure than he thinks.

A hooked fish will instantly begin to run or leap, and the angler counters by immediately tightening up his line. If he is in the water he should start backing off to get on land or in very shallow water, and he should begin to work to get to the downstream side of his fish. The angler's purpose should be to turn the fish to face downstream, and the angler should try to do his fighting from dry land where he can manuever best. The fish's natural instinct will be to run away from the point of contact so that the angler then works in behind the fish and with pressure, turns the fish so that it heads downstream. A big one will put on all kinds of acrobatics and will fight with the steady determination of a bull. It will take runs upstream, across stream and may go racing downstream with the angler forced to scamper after it, often tripping and bumping over rocks for 100 yards or more, but eventually when the run is over the fish will turn and face upstream again. The angler's fighting should again manuever to get on the downstream side of the fish and again exert pressure from behind the fish to turn him downstream. The water coming into a fish's gill from upstream gives the fish oxygen, but on a downstream run this oxygen is reduced and it helps to tire a fish. How well this works is illustrated by the fact that top notch anglers like Don Leyden consider 1 minute per pound ample time necessary to wear a fish down to a point where it's ready for landing.

When the fish is ready to be landed the angler knows, for the salmon will act and look tired. The fish will be wobbling from side to side and its gills will be opening and closing, looking like a man breathing heavy. Whenever a fish is still making hard straight runs the angler should keep fighting the fish until it is tired enough to be led. Some anglers will try to take a fresh fish, but this is dangerous and it is far more sporty to fight them until they are worn out—sometimes just one more run of a minute or less will make all the difference in the world between a fresh fish opposed to a tired one. Don waits because fresh fish are the ones that are lost in landing, while a tired salmon can be led to landing like a docile sheep.

Landing is always a dangerous time with all fish, but with Atlantic salmon it is more precarious because of their size and the light tackle most anglers generally use. Any fish making a sudden lunge, run or dive, may rip a hook from its mouth or part a leader as easy as if it were spider threads. Don wants his fish tired when he brings him in, and he wants him so tired that if necessary, he could beach the fish, which he has done on some occasions. If the fish were fresh it just couldn't be led right into shallow water of two or three inches, and then right to the beach itself where it can be picked up by hand. A fresh fish would flip and break off the line, but a truly tired fish can simply be "dragged" right out of the water.

Most of the time Don and other salmon anglers land their fish by leading them into the big two handed landing nets that are especially made for the purpose. As this fishing is done with the aid of a guide, it is generally the guide's job to assist an angler in taking a fish. Often a guide will come up behind a fish and simply try to net him from behind. This will work alright if the fish is tired, but it can cause some fine fireworks if he isn't a "pooped-out" fish. Fisherman Leyden wants his guides merely to put the net down into the water holding it on a 45 degree angle up from the bottom and then holding it still. He doesn't want the guide to do another thing but lift the net when the fish is safely inside it. Don says, "If the fish is tired he will follow my line right into the net never trying to veer off or run away. If he isn't tired and does veer off, I will have enough line out so there is no danger of parting the line by a sudden rush. Then I have the guide stand still while I fight the fish some more, and then lead him right into the stationary net. This way I land the fish with a minimum chance of losing it during landing."

Don recalls a recent trip on which he was fishing alone in a stretch of water when he hooked into a beauty, and had a fine tug of war with him. Don shouted back to camp and the only guide left was one he had never worked with. By the time the guide entered the water the fish was looking tired and the guide started to get behind the fish. Don quickly told him just what he wanted him to do and although the guide did it, it was obvious his heart wasn't in it. The first time the fish veered off and ran across the stream and Don could almost feel the growing question in the guide's mind. This was a dangerous stretch of water to be playing with this big fish, for there was an extremely shallow bar on the opposite side where a fish could easily be lost. Still he told the guide to stay put and he played the big salmon around, keeping it away from the bar and finally leading him in again. This time the fish went right into the net just as if it were trained to do it. When the guide lifted up this beauty that went over 20 pounds he turned to Don Leyden, grinned and said, "Mister, yuz is awful easy to net a fish for." Don never forgot those words for he feels a fish should always be easy to net, or it is just not ready for netting.

There is one other way many anglers land their fish, and that it with a tailer. This is a stick with a wire rope that is made into kind of a lasso. The object here is to slip the noose over the tail of the fish, bringing it up in front of the adipose fin. The angler or guide then lifts his hand thus tightening the loop around the tail of the salmon and lifting the fish right out of the water tail first. Don feels tailers are fine for landing salmon, but he warns that once the motion of lifting is begun it must be done in one quick steady swoop without a second's hesitation. The salmon have tremendous power in their tails and he has seen them knock the tailers right out of guides' hands. He even saw a fish break a tailer when it wasn't administered correctly. However, when the guide or angler knows how to use one they are excellent and offer the extra advantage in that the upside down fish is temporarily paralyzed, thus making him completely still while being held.

When everything is done perfectly from hookup to landing, a fish will always be taken, but because this is a sport where the unexpected often happens many fish are lost. Don Leyden says sometimes an angler will lose one fish, then another and still another and he will go into a fishing slump. He says, "After a while you begin to wonder—how am I going to lose this one?" This is just like the baseball batter who gets into a slump—he has to work his way out of it and get that bad mental picture out of his mind. Don recalls once over 5 years ago he went into a terrible slump and by actual count missed 14 hooked fish in a row. This happened by every conceivable method, through parted lines, spit hooks, rough water, landing, and on and on. He did the only thing possible—gritted his teeth and began to try to work his way out of this state. After a few successes his touch came back and today he lands most of the fish he hooks, and losses are the unusual. But this shows that even the best anglers can get into a slump where the only way out is hard work and keeping heart.

Don Leyden's Atlantic salmon fishing tackle generally consists of a 9 foot rod of medium action. He is against using the overly large rods, simply because they are unwieldy. His line is weight forward line, generally WF 8, which gives him extra casting distance. Nine feet of thin diameter 6 pound test tapered leader are added to the line to give the fly complete deception on its float.

The flies which are the most important part of the tackle have in the last few years changed considerably. Don has always tied his own flies and he has hundreds of them at his home that vary from the long colorful traditional salmon flies down to the very small ones that in many respects look no different from trout flies in common use. During the last five years he and a group of salmon anglers have developed their own theories concerning salmon flies which have greatly reduced the number of patterns an angler has to take with him on any trip. These patterns have been reduced down to a point where they now feel an angler could fish with as little as two basic flies; the Squirrel Tail, a silhouette fly, and the Valdon, an actual vision fly. Add a few variations of these basic patterns, tie them in varying sizes, and that would be all the flies anyone would need to Atlantic salmon fish on the Miramichi.

The squirrel tail fly and its various derivitives are silhouette flies which are best used whenever light conditions are bright. When the sunlight hits the water, its broken surface deflects the light rays. The result is that the fish in the water can only see silhouettes of objects that may be on the surface of the water. To illustrate the point hold a fly up to a bright or florescent light, and when looking at it only the outline of the fly will be visible with bright light right behind it. The salmon have no eyelids, but they compensate by positioning themselves in such a way as to hide their eyes from the harshest rays of the light, yet on bright conditions all that they can see above them will be the silhouettes. Thus, when an insect lands on the water the fish will move up at the silhouette as he had done as a paar. The fisherman's job is to make his fly appear just the way these insects appear to the salmon.

The various squirrel tail flies very closely resemble each other. To show how similar they are the Black Squirrel Tail is the same as the Squirrel Tail except the wing is made of Black Squirrel Tail instead of canadian Pine Squirrel Tail. Don's favorite is the Green Butt Squirrel Tail which is simply a Black Squirrel Tail tied with some green nylon wool for a butt. These squirrel tail flies create a silhouette that is very similar to the silhouette created by the basic insect of this area—the stone fly. These flies produce excellent results because the salmon, as young fish, were oriented to hit at these flies whenever they saw one.

The second group of flies, the Valdons, are the ones that are used when the light is not bright, and the surface is not rippling. These are best whenever the fish get a clear unobstructed view of the fly. Where once hundreds of types with thousands of color variations were thought essential for actual vision flies, these sophisticated salmon anglers have advanced to a point where with a few patterns they are able to fish continually. Don Leyden and his group of anglers feel that by constructing actual vision flies that utilize natural prismatic feathers, they can get better results than they did when they made hundreds of patterns out of dyed feathers.

A prismatic feather is one that will act like a prism, and when light hits it will appear as if every color of the rainbow is in that feather. The most important single feather in a Valdon fly is the wing feather, which is constructed of a wild turkey body feather. Although a wild turkey feather may appear black at first glance, when it is seen in the light colors will pour out of it. Hold one of these feathers and view it. It is truly a beautiful thing, for against its black background every color of the rainbow is visible. In the water the feather functions the same way, so where anglers once switched from blue feathers, to green ones, to red ones and so on now they get better results with one fly that in effect duplicates many colors.

The fly tier uses natural material when obtainable for the most parts of all flies. These create a much more life-like reproduction than the flies tied with opaque dyed materials. Don Leyden says, "The English Blue Game Hackles, with their magnificient brilliance and shading, make these flies 'come alive' when used in their dressings."

Both the silhouette and natural vision flies are best fished wet, and the object is to drift them just under the surface of the water. The angler should ride a fly 1 to 4 inches under the surface of the water for best results. Flies presented perfectly will raise fish from 4 to 6 feet of water regularly, and sometimes may even raise one from a depth of up to 10 feet.

Although these two basic patterns will take fish on the Miramichi under many conditions, still the size of the fly used is always important. Generally speaking, 90% of all the salmon fishing will be done with flies tied on No. 4, 6 or 8 hooks, while larger or smaller hooks are used in extreme conditions.

The large fiies, the No. 4's (and for extreme conditions up to No. 2's) will be used when the water is high or when the water is very cold. Also they may be used if the fish are very deep or they are very big. Big fish are harder to raise as they have been away from feeding on insects for a long time, therefore it is often difficult to bring out this latent instinct. Another time for large flies is when the water is very bright and generally large flies are used whenever the fish are not anxious to rise to a fly.

Small sized flies are called for whenever the water is warm and low, the sky is overcast, and the fish's vision is not bothered by glare. The small sized flies will go to No. 8's (and on extreme occasions down to No. 12's) and they have the advantage of giving a more accurate reproduction of the local insect life. They are best when the fish are active and will readily rise to a fly.

There are, of course, occasions when these anglers will switch from these two basic patterns. Sometimes they switch off simply for variety, but occasionally there may be a perfectly logical reason for this. Where the Miramichi water is crystal clear, the water of one of its tributaries the Cains is cedar colored. Here the anglers will fish bright flies like the Oriole or gold bodied flies. Sometimes for the sake of sport, the anglers will switch to one of the big hairy dry flies. Here Mr. Leyden warns that they do not raise the fish very well and to get action the angler must get his fly directly over a fish. He warns that dry flies should never be fished blind, but should only be used where the angler can see the fish.

To Don Leyden fishing and the outdoors is a way of life—it is being with nature and enjoying life in its fullest. He loves salmon fishing more than any other sport, yet he is an excellent hunter among whose prizes include a wild turkey whose feathers are in his Valdon flies, he formerly held the International Game Fish Association world record having taken a 29 pound 12 ounce pollack on 12 pound test line, and he is a striper fisherman who knows how to take a big one. Donald Leyden loves many phases of outdoor sports yet the demanding skill of fly fishing for the majestic Atlantic salmon is where he really excels.

Name	*Squirrel Tail*	*Black Squirrel Tail*	*Squirrel Tail Green Butt*	*Squirrel Tail Orange Tag*	*Valdon*	*Gold Valdon*
Tail	Red Nylon Strands	Red Nylon Strands	Green Nylon Strands	Red Nylon Strands	Rusty Dun Fiber Tail	Honey Dun Tail
Tag	None	None	None	Orange Silk	Red Silk	Orange Silk
Butt	None	None	Green Florescent Wool	Orange Florescent Wool	Florescent Red	Florescent Orange
Body	Black Nylon Wool Ribbed With Silver Tinsel	Black Nylon Wool Ribbed With Silver Tinsel	Black Nylon Wool Ribbed With Silver Tinsel	Black Nylon Wool Ribbed With Silver Tinsel	Silver Tinsel Ribbed With Silver Wire	Gold Tinsel Ribbed With Gold Wire
Hackle	Rusty Dun (Black)	Rusty Dun (Black)	Rusty Dun (Black)	Rusty Dun (Black)	Rusty Dun (Black)	Honey Dun
Wing	Squirrel	Black Squirrel	Black Squirrel	Under Wing of Golden Phesants Tippets Main Wing of Black Squirrel	Sparse Black Squirrel Underwing Wild Turkey Wing	Sparse Pine Squirrel Underwing Bronze Barred Wild Turkey Wing
Hook Sizes	No. 4 to 8	No. 4 to 8	No. 4 to 8	No. 4 to 8	No. 4 to 8	No. 4 to 8
Imitation	Stone Fly	Stone Fly	Stone Fly	Stone Fly	Insect With Color	Insect With Color
Fly Type	Silhouette	Silhouette	Silhouette	Silhouette	Actual Vision	Actual Vision
Best Use	Bright Light	Bright Light	Bright Light	Bright Light	Dull Light	Dull Light

2. BASS FISHING WITH JIMMY HOLT

Angler Jimmy Holt has been catching bass out of T.V.A. lakes with carefree abandon since 1950 and he feels what the State of Tennessee now needs is more anglers to catch more and bigger fish to better balance the bass population of these fecund waters. Unlike so many other top anglers of our country, Jimmy states that the fish population of the T.V.A. states has grown so rapidly that it would be perfectly safe to double the 10 bass a day legal limit.

Tennessee is ringed by T.V.A. and Corps of Engineering flood control lakes—22 in all with two new ones under construction. They constitute thousands of miles of freshwater impoundments that range in size from 900 acre Davy Crockett Lake to huge 158,300 acre Kentucky Lake which has 2,380 miles of shoreline in Tennessee and Kentucky. Other impoundments are in Alabama, Missouri, Florida, Georgia, North Carolina, South Carolina, Texas and Oklahoma. Thus there has been a fish population explosion throughout this whole area. Tennesseans feel they are the center of this fishing, and just to illustrate the extent of the fishing, the world record smallmouth bass, an 11 pound, 15 ounce whopper, came from Dale Hollow Lake which is in Tennessee and Kentucky. The walleye record, a 25 pounder, came from Old

Hickory Lake, Tennessee, and the water below Dale Hollow reservoir produced a 26 pound, 2 ounce brown trout which held the North American record for several years. The lakes of this state have produced some largemouth bass approaching 20 pounds, and sportsman Jimmy Holt is sure that in these lakes there are bass larger than the 22 pound, 4 ounce world record fish from Montgomery Lake in Georgia.

These reservoirs offer excellent sauger fishing and the bluegill and crappie fishing is second to none. Also catfish are gigantic here and in the water below Pickwick Dam there is an annual derby where fish over 100 pounds have been taken. Jimmy Holt, on very rare occasions, stops to fish for anything other than bass as this is his fish and he pursues them relentlessly all year long.

This angler was introduced to bass fishing by his brother, Jack over 18 years ago. He recalls back in those days the standard way was to get a batch of plugs, head out for the water and work the shoreline. They used to skull around mostly taking turns doing the skulling, but Jimmy admits in his early fishing days it was his brother who did most of the work, in fact, he recalls it was his brother who gave him his first outboard motor saying, "Now you can go out by yourself."

Jimmy recalls they had some real fine productive fishing days and some of the plugs worked wonders. He still has a few of them among the hundreds he keeps in his work shop which is his fishing tackle haven. Plugs, he recalls, were a challenging way for catching bass, but today the fishing tackle industry has produced lures which will take bass under all conditions, seasons and times of day.

He says, "There have been changes in every phase of fishing, including tackle, boats, motors, lures, and even in the waters themselves. Fishing here has improved radically in every way, and best of all I think we are far from the end for shortly there will be even better bass fishing than there is now.

"One of the really important advances in developing productive bass fishing methods is that anglers have learned to use the jig. In our deep water reservoirs including Center Hill and Dale

Hollow, they are currently the most extensively used lures by the anglers that are catching the biggest and most fish in this area. The favorite jig here is the Doll-Fly made by Thompson Fishing Tackle Company of Knoxville, Tennessee. There are, of course, many similar jigs, but I have had such tremendous success with this one that I tend to stick with it. Basically it is a simple jig with a painted lead head of any color you choose and long strands of yellow, black or white bear hair covering a 2/0 to 3/0 hook, depending on the size of the jig.

"Now if an angler just goes out and fishes this jig he will take some bass with it, but where we differ is we add a piece of pork rind to the jig. The rind is hooked right onto the hook and the tail is left trailing. Then when the jig moves through the water, the pork rind with a little rod movement will come alive, and any bass that is near it will take a taste.

"We have found that ordinary white pork rind will take bass during the spring months, and that black rind works even better on certain days—it's a trial and error method. My best luck has been using a 3-inch rind either white, black or yellow. I like a 3-inch piece where the tail splits into two trailing pieces. Our choice is Pedigo's Pork rind made by Cicil Pedigo Pork Rind Co. of Bowling Green, Kentucky.

"The strange thing about this fishing is that we have developed our own methods for fishing a jig. When I start a day of fishing in a deep and clear lake such as Dale Hollow, I generally like to work a shoreline. I prefer to first work the bank on out to about 20 feet offshore. I maneuver my boat so that it is 30 to 40 feet from the point I'm casting to and I throw my loaded jig right into the shoreline. I use a 1/8 ounce jig for this fishing. When my lure hits the water I begin reeling in immediately, allowing the jig to sink slowly. I bring the jig back to the boat in a slow steady motion, trying to keep the jig close to the bottom at all times. This of course gets tricky because the banks are steep and drop off rapidly in many places and the angler must allow for this drop being sure his jig is near the bottom. If the retrieve is too fast you don't get the action and if it is too slow, you'll be hung up most of the time. To do this properly takes practice. Once the angler gets experience he will mentally be able to envision just where his jig is at all times during the retrieve. This light ⅛ ounce jig is also tremendously effective on the flats where the water may be 3 feet deep at its deepest point.

"The other significant point is to know the shoreline. The jig-rind combination, like every other bait or lure, has to be fished where the fish are to get catches. When I fish a jig I cast it right into the shore or in next to the grass or weeds. If there is an old log in the water my jig goes right at it or when there are some stumps I throw 5 feet beyond so that my retrieve runs right by the stump. When working these hotspots the retrieve is slow and easy in a steady motion. If the bass is there, he will hit it and will hit hard.

"Whenever the bass are inshore and I work my jigs, I have no problem getting them to hit. They really go for this combination. Of course the light ⅛ ounce jig is best during the early morning, the evening or the springtime when the bass are most likely to be on the shoreline. It makes for great fishing."

This angler explains, if he fishes for ½ hour along the shore and gets nothing, or nothing more than 1 or 2 small ones, he then knows it is time to move offshore slightly and fish in somewhat deeper water. He says, "I still stay with the jig-rind but instead of a ⅛ ounce jig I will use a ¼ ounce lure. This goes down faster and is better in deeper water. This lure is most effective when the fish are in water 10 to 20 feet deep. I know many of the bluffs where the fish go when they slip off the shoreline, or I'll go into one of the bigger creeks along the lake. Here I will cast my combination out and let it sink until it gets to the bottom, and then I retrieve slow and easily along the bottom bouncing the jig and stirring a little mud to arouse the fish. Bass go for the jig-rind and the important thing is to be sure to have the bait working slowly near the bottom. If it is placed near a bass he will take it and will hit hard."

Jimmy explains when a bass hits the angler will feel a real bump and that's the time to lift the rod tip to set the hook deep.

Some fish come right up to the surface leaping out and making every effort to spit the hook. What starts as an underwater hit may end as a tremendous surface battle, and sometimes its up and down again with the fish digging for the bottom ledges or underwater brush, but no matter what happens it's excitement all the way until a fish is landed.

When the fish are really deep during winter months the 3/8 ounce jig-rind is fished in the deep holes of the lake and this has proved an excellent way of taking bass. During the summer months the fish will also be in deep holes, or whenever there is lots of activity such as boating or water skiing they tend to go down. They will still take a bait, but an angler must get it down to them because they will not come up. Also, during cold weather when the water temperature is under 45 degrees largemouth bass have a tendency to drop down deep, and the only way to get them is to go after them.

When fishing a 3/8 ounce jig, Jimmy suggests the angler cast out and then give the jig plenty of time to sink to the bottom. Once the line is on the bottom, the retrieve is begun by reeling in very slowly, always making sure the lure stays on or near the bottom. This angler will sometimes lift the rod tip and drop it, making the jig bounce along the bottom in standard jig fashion. If he gets one this way, he calls it "hand shaking 'em on." Making the jig bounce is not essential for a slow steady moving lure right over the bottom is what brings him the most hits.

Jimmy says, "Originally it was hard to convince me to swing over to the jigs. I had always been a bass plug man, and once the angler is stuck on one type of lure he is hesitant to change. Then I saw some of the fantastic catches some anglers were getting and I felt I had to try them. At first I took some along but never really gave them a chance, since I would fish a jig a few minutes, get disgusted and go right back to plugging. This went on for some time, I of course was catching fish, but I was regularly being out fished by other anglers, so finally I decided to give the jigs a real try. I went on a weekend fishing trip to Centre Hill Lake and took nothing but jigs and pork rinds with me. I fished for two solid days with this combination. On the first day the pickings were lean as I was experimenting and was just getting the feel of them. However, on the second day I took my limit of 10 bass and three of these fish were over 5 pounds each while the others were all over 2 pounds. I was hooked and I have been fishing this combination as my primary method ever since—it has really paid off. I found it takes time to get the right retrieve every cast, but once you get into a good'un you then have it made."

Last fall Jimmy began experimenting again and instead of using a jig-pork rind combination he tried a jig-plastic worm combination. He says, "I took one good sized bass with the jig-plastic worm late in November and I feel that it should work just as well as the jig-pork rind. The plastic worm I used was a big 7 incher that was a deep purple color so I imagine in the water this combination didn't look any different than the jig-pork rind and would work just as well under all circumstances. I plan to do much more fishing with the jig-worm combo this year."

The other method of fishing that has really improved the bass catches of Tennessee anglers is fishing the plastic worms. This fishing has of course received tremendous amounts of publicity, but top bass angler Jimmy Holt feels the worms couldn't be publicized enough as they are really producers.

He says, "In Tennessee we fish only the large plastic worms, those 6 inches or more with some anglers using them as long as 10 inches. I generally stick to worms about 7 inches in length and I get the kind that do not have hooks in them. I insert my own 3/0 or 4/0 hook into the worm by pushing the hook right through the head of the worm and then out of the body about 1½ inches down. I insert the point and barb of the hook back into the worm leaving them buried in the body of the worm. This makes the lure weedless as there is nothing protruding that can catch the weeds. This is a fine method of fishing Kentucky Lake or Woods Reservoir which are shallow and weedy.

"Sometimes when I'm fishing in areas where I know I will

have no snagging problems I rig them in a standard fashion running the hook approximately ⅓ the way through the worm and out. I use only one hook in a worm because I find the fish that hit the tail of the worm are generally bluegill, crappie or small bass. When a big bass wants the worm he takes the whole thing."

This angler explains that the plastic worms should have about ⅛ or ¼ ounce egg sinker on the line, running free, in front of the hook when the angler fishes deep. This will give plenty of weight to get down 15 feet or more to dig out the fish. The worms are fished by casting the lure out and giving it plenty of time to get down to the bottom and then very slowly retrieving. The main thing with the worms is to move them ever so slowly because they are so much more effective when moved at practically a snail's pace.

When the fish are in the shallows, the barrel weight is removed and one or two pieces of split shot are added to the line about a foot above the hook. These will add a little weight and take the worm down enough in shallow water. The worms are fished pretty much the same manner as the jigs, for they are cast right to the shore and retrieved painfully slow. If there are weeds about Jimmy will cast right into them or cast right into other obstructions. When the water is high and up around the buck bushes, bass will hide beneath them and when a worm is cast past a bush and worked back around the root it is as Jimmy Holt says, "A bass will hit or die trying."

The area between two stumps or weed beds are good spots to spend time working over. Stumps, sunken logs and other underwater obstructions add up to excellent hot spots. Jimmy suggests that the angler cast slightly beyond the spot and then make sure that the worm will pass right over or by the obstruction on the retrieve.

Bass hit the worms several ways, but generally the big fish really attack. This is great, because one second that fish is hooked and the next second he may be jumping through the ozone trying to spit the hook. This angler explains that other times the bass will grab the worm and run with it. He then lets the line out freely and begins counting and watching and when he thinks the bass really has the worm he lifts the rodtip and strikes the hook. If the fish only seems to play with the worm, then Jimmy Holt waits about 15 seconds and then lifts the rodtip to strike. He gets many fish this way, but he loses some too.

Angler Jimmy Holt feels these are the best producing methods developed to date. He says. "When a new lure or bait is produced I will try it as I enjoy experimenting, but when they don't prove out I quickly go back to my regular producing lures and methods."

He explains that there are many live bait anglers in Tennessee. They can generally be divided into two distinct groups—the anglers that fish with minnows and the spring lizard fishermen. The minnow fishermen will fish in the coves and along the shore, but they generally have their best results when they go to the head of the lakes and fish big minnows. Their best results are in the spring of the year, and in fact, the 25 pound world record walleye was taken by a local angler fishing this method. This can be productive fishing, and one only has to take a look at the sizes of some of the fish these anglers take to see its worth.

The other group of live baiters are the spring lizard fishermen. They get out in the lakes and cast a salamander or other type of lizard to the weeds or other hotspots. Some of them now attach their lizard to a lead head jig and work it back the same way a jig-rind is worked. These live bait anglers will use all kinds of edible food as bait, but the spring lizards are among their favorites. They do very well too, and the best time for this fishing is in the spring when the weather gets real hot. Jimmy doesn't care for live bait angling, as he prefers using lures since they offer more activity and they are more productive, or as he says, "At least for me they are."

Through the years this angler has tried about every plug made, and in fact, has made many of his own. He loves plug fishing and today will spend much time fishing plugs whenever he feels conditions warrant it.

One plug he is fond of is a Fred Arbogast Bait Co., Sputterfuss. This is a metal plug with a propeller in front of its flat metal head. He says, "This plug sinks, but it is most effective fished along the surface so that it creates a surface disturbance. A good fishing buddy told me to use it and I added a piece of pork rind trailing. It is weedless and I like to fish it in the weeds and in the shallow water. This is an excellent plug to use on nesting fish as it really stirs them up. The tricky part is that the cast has to be made and the retrieve begun the very second the lure hits the water as the Sputterfuss should not be permitted to sink. I begin by reeling it in immediately and will continue bringing it in at a pace fast enough to keep the lure at the surface. This keeps the spinner buzzing and brings the bass up mad. Often it will be splash-whamo! Some bass go out of their minds trying to devour that chunk of metal."

He feels that under correct circumstances all the tested standard plugs produce well including the Flatfish, Arbogaster Bomber, Rapala, Jitterbug and other popular favorites. One point he makes is about the currently popular Rapala which he feels has a fine motion moving through the water and is a real fish catcher, but he feels it is such a light plug that it really can't be cast on windy days. He says, "It is something that we learned early that almost all plugs are best worked slowly. Most top water lures are most effective when twitched on the surface moving and moved slowly, while underwater plugs should be moved at the speed of a leisurely moving fish." (Among the plugs he has a special place for in his tackle box are the Arbogaster Bomber, and the Swimming Minnow as they netted him some of his best catches).

This angler recalls one day he was fishing a Swimming Minnow at Center Hill Reservoir in East Tennessee about 70 miles from Nashville. He says, "It was December and it was spitting snow on and off and it was so cold my hands were numb. I know it's generally best to work deep in cold weather and I had been, but I had a feeling and began fishing in a relatively shallow creek. I cast my Swimming Minnow and something came up and smashed the lure and just from the way it hit I knew it was big. The fish headed for deep water and it was a tug-of-war. I finally got it in to my big long handed landing net and the fish turned out to be a $10\frac{1}{2}$ pound largemouth taken by fishing completely against the book.

"Book fishing says go deep for big bass and it also says go down for largemouth bass when the weather gets cold. I was fishing in three feet of water and there were patches of snow all over the shore while ice was forming in my rod guides. I will fish against the book anytime because I believe a lot of fishing is a sixth sense. Anytime an angler feels that he can catch a fish in a place he should fish it because it has been my experience that when I get that feeling I usually get one. The reverse is also true for if I feel I'm not going to get one—I get out for the chances are I will be wasting my time in that spot.

"There are certain basic differences in fishing for smallmouth bass as opposed to largemouth bass. The one most essential difference is that smallmouth are very active in cold water while largemouth bass will get sluggish. When the water temperatures of the lakes gets down around 45 degrees during the winters, the smallmouths get just as active as could be. Anytime between October and April Dale Hollow is probably the finest single smallmouth bass lake in the country, especially for big smallmouth. Dale Hollow is of course famous because the world record smallmouth was taken there, but I think Center Hill, a little further South, which is not quite as well known outside the state, is equally as good a smallmouth lake. As a matter of fact, Center Hill, has been my best lake as I took my biggest smallmouth, a 7 pounder there. That fish jumped, twisted and battled all the way—a tremendously exciting fish. My personal opinion is that in April and May this is the easiest lake in the world to take bass as the fishing is so productive then.

"These Northeastern Tennessee impoundments hold the water rushing down from the hills and the water is cold. The water here is mountain spring clear most of the time, and when I'm fishing in 20 feet of water I can look down and still see my lure. The lakes are very deep and the water stays cool all year making them perfect for smallmouth. The water released from the bottom of the lakes through the dams is cold enough to support brown and rainbow trout and extensive fishing for them goes on. Here the fish that held the North American Brown trout record for several years was taken."

Minnesota lakes and upstate New York in the Thousand Islands area have their best smallmouth fishing in the early summer when the water temperatures there go to 40 to 50 degrees. Jimmy explains Tennessee gets these water temperatures in the fall and spring and consequently their best smallmouth fishing is then. Their fish get larger than those of the Northern water because Tennessee doesn't get freeze-overs which put the fish down in the mud and off feed. He says, "Our fish can feed and fatten up all year long and consequently they grow big.

"My methods of fishing and my baits are quite similar for both smallmouth and largemouth bass. In methods, one difference is that I fish much more open water for smallmouth as these fish have less of a tendency to hide under stumps and logs and prefer more open water. They will often be along weed beds or along the dropoff of ledges on the lakes.

"The seasons I fish smallmouth are completely opposite the largemouth seasons for my serious smallmouth fishing begins in the fall, continue right through the winter and into the spring. I generally do not fish smallmouth during the summers, other than at night because when the surface temperature of the water exceeds 60 degrees these fish become sluggish. You can sometimes catch one and hardly get any fight at all out of it. Other smallmouth dig down so low during the hot summers that they go 50 to 100 feet deep."

One of the many interesting fishing contests held in the state was a frozen fisherman's contest held at Center Hill in December, but not being held now. A few years ago Jimmy Holt fished 30 hours from daylight to dusk in one of these contests and took 18 small mouth bass in two days. The biggest fish weighed 5 pounds, and every one of them were charged with vitality. He took second place for his five pounder. Jimmy says, "I love winter fishing as it is the best time for smallmouth and it is a time when I have miles of lake all to myself and I can really enjoy the eloquence of solitude on these beautiful lakes."

Largemouth bass fishing takes on a completely opposite picture for as the water temperatures go below 45 degrees these fish slow up. Then the more the water temperatures drop, the more likely largemouth are to just sink into the mud. In the cold water these fish will be half dead on the hook offering little challenge. However, in the spring the largemouth get active fast and at the first sign of the water warming they swarm all over the shoreline. The bull bass and the females are vicious then, attacking anything in the area of their breeding places and any angler can go into some coves or creeks and catch his ten fish limit. He explains that if the chamber of commerce offered every fisherman visiting the state a money back guarantee if he didn't take some bass, it wouldn't cost them a dime. Jimmy can't imagine how anyone could miss taking largemouth bass when the fish are in the shallow water and when they will take any plug, lure or bait with reckless abandon.

The beauty of largemouths is that they stay active from Spring until late Fall and during the summers warm water never bothers them a bit. When the water surface temperatures go past 75 degrees largemouths will never be affected as the fish are just as vigorous then as when the water is 55 degrees.

The largemouth bass love to hide by obstructions until they see an edible bait, and then they strike. They get next to, or under, old stumps, under logs, floats and boat docks, or they hide in weeds. The fish spend much of their time in shallow water and some of the best spots are the shallow creeks that empty into the lakes. Jimmy says, "I have taken more bass in less than 3 feet of water than from any other depth and I've taken a great number in water less than a foot in depth."

The habits of the bass are easy to learn and the next logical thing for catching largemouths is knowing the spots along the shore that are productive. On large lakes whenever the water level goes down, Jimmy will take his camera to the lake and shoot pictures of the shoreline. This is best when the level is down 6 to 8 feet or more as the old stumps, shallow ledges that will be weedbeds in the spring will be out of water. Later the angler can use the pictures to identify the productive places and he can fish them.

"One thing I have learned about fishing in this state, especially Kentucky Lake and that is when I am working a shoreline and I happen to see a canepole sticking up out in the water, I fish that spot thoroughly. The lakes here are huge and it is often difficult to find a hot spot a second time, so many anglers solve this by marking the stump rows in some manner. I consider it better than even money that there will be some good fishing stumps holding some big bass within ten feet of a cane pole marking."

This sportsman explains that Old Hickory Lake, Kentucky Lake, Barkley Lake and Laurel Hill Lake of Western Tennessee are all primarily largemouth bass lakes. These are essentially shallow lakes and in many sections outside of the channel markers the water is extremely shallow over vast areas. This is excellent water for largemouth bass and any angler who has a week's time in April, May, or June could in all probability catch the legal limit of ten largemouth a day varying from 2 pounds on up.

One interesting phenomenon recently occurred on a new lake, Lake Barkley, which is a recent impoundment of the Cumberland River. This lake, although not as big as Kentucky Lake parallels it, running North and South through Tennessee and Kentucky for many miles. There is a canal connecting the two lakes and when Barkley Lake was 1 year old there was a bass, crappie and bluegill population explosion of an unbelievable degree. Many anglers were going there and hooking 100 to 200 bass in a day. Most of the bass, over the ten fish a day limit, were released, but nevertheless it made for fantastic action. Anglers were going for bass using barbless hooks and lures that had never produced before were working wonders—it was a real paradise.

This new lake had its original fish from those that were in the river while others came through the canal. Millions of fingerlings were here and when the lake filled up there was such a tremendous supply of food and no competition for the young fish that they grew at an absolutely unbelievable rate. Virtually the entire hatches of fingerlings grew and thrived. The fish caught were never big fish, but generally going 1 or 2 pounds. According to conservationists this phenomena is not unusual so Jimmy tells fishermen to keep their eyes open for new lakes as in all probability there will be a fish population explosion there. The Cumberland River is currently being dammed in another section and Jimmy Holt is anxious to see the results as this is in a smallmouth bass section of the river.

There is one other type of bass, the Kentucky Bass—a hybrid of a large and smallmouth bass. These fish do not come big as they seldom reach 5 pounds in Tennessee, but they are good and sporty. The Kentucky bass stay active in summer and in the water it acts like a smallmouth bass while physically it more closely appears like a largemouth. The Kentucky bass has a short stocky body and has a half dozen rows of small black spots below the lateral line running along its body. Sometimes it is extremely difficult to tell this fish from other bass and on occasion Jimmy has to put his finger in the fish's mouth to finally determine if it is a Kentucky bass. These bass have small teeth all over their tongue.

Jimmy Holt feels that the 10 a day bass limit in Tennessee could very well be raised to 20 fish a day without ever denting the bass population of the state. He feels that very few fishermen actually ever string 10 bass a day as most average anglers only get the limit on one or two spring trips when the fish are in the spawning beds. He explains even the best anglers don't get the limit on every trip during a year, possibly averaging 5 or 6 fish a trip, so that the increased limit would hardly put a dent in the ever growing bass population. He explains that there are no limits on crappie or bluegill and these fish are really thriving.

Mr. Holt explains that although he does most of his fishing in Tennessee and Kentucky every once in a while he does like to break out and see what other areas have to offer in the way of bass fishing. One trip that really impressed him was to Lake Seminole in Southern Georgia. This lake is a huge flooded forest. It is a series of creeks running through the area and the remainder being flooded flatlands with extremely shallow water that has stumps and trees covered with Spanish moss everywhere. It is almost always fished with a guide because an angler could easily get lost forever. Jimmy fished it with and without a guide, but he admits he took some careful compass readings the first time he went out alone. The number and size of the largemouth bass in Lake Seminole are really fantastic. He tells of one stretch of 20 minutes of fishing where he took four bass weighing from 5 to 9½ pounds each The biggest was the 9½ pounder which turned out to be a real Confederate Cavalry fighter. All four fish, he explains were taken on a Bushwacker with the piece of pork rind added. The Bushwacker is nothing more than a single spinner with a bucktail and a hook.

Much of the equipment Jimmy uses he makes himself. He has made plugs and other lures that took fish, but what he really enjoys is making his own rods. He feels that manufactured rods simply do not measure up to what he wants in a bass fishing rod. His own rods are custom tailored to a very special use and are made with the very finest of materials and painstaking work. He uses either Lamaglass or Grisley for the rod and he likes rods approximately 5½ to 6 feet in length of single piece construction. The handles on his rods are made with cork. Jimmy builds his rods as one piece for he feels a ferrule throws off the action of a rod and the few rods he made in his life of two piece construction the ferrule was placed within six inches of the grip so that the arch of the rod would not be disturbed in fighting a fish. Another innovation of a Holt bass rod is that it has six rod guides and a tip, whereas almost all manufactured rods have four or five guides and a tip. Jimmy will readily demonstrate the difference the extra guides make for when pressure is put on the line it distributes it evenly over the whole rod instead of at a few pressure points. This gives the angler a better rod in a fight with a fish as the rod will take considerable strain off the line. He says, "I demonstrated my ideas on rods for years and talked to many anglers about it. I made some rods for friends and they were really impressed when they used them. I think my idea is finally catching on for recently I saw where one manufacturer came out with a six guide rod for bass fishing.

Jimmy fishes two types of rods and brings both types with him on almost all fishing trips. He fishes a spinning rod with an open faced Mitchell 300 or 308 reel holding 6 pound monofilament line whenever he is in relatively open water like that found at Center Hill or Dale Hollow Lakes. He likes this best as it is light line fishing which tests the skill of an angler against a big fish. However, when he fishes in the canals and around obstructions he knows the first thing a big hooked bass will do is to dive for one of the obstructions and then it's "goodby Mr. Bass." Therefore, when fishing in and around dangerous water he uses a baitcasting rod, also with 6 guides, and he couples this with an Ambassador 5000 casting reel holding 14 pound test line. With this combination he has a better chance to hurry the fish out into open water where he can enjoy the hardest fighting bass there are.

The Tennessee lakes and other Southern impoundments are large and the boats and motors used by many anglers are specialized for this kind of fishing. Every conceivable type of boat in existence from a small rowboat to 60 foot cruisers will appear on the lakes. However, anglers have certain needs they want met and Jimmy feels that his boat, a Boston Whaler, is just suited for this fishing. This is a flat bottomed tri-hedral hull boat of glass that has a shallow draft. The boat is powered by a 55 horse Chrysler engine and can literally fly over the water while it can also be guided into the shallow creeks and coves making it excellent for both purposes.

His boat, and others like it have two bucket seats, one up front and the other in the rear. It utilizes two motors, the powerful running motor in the rear and an electric fishing motor up front. When fishing, the almost perfectly silent electric motor is used as it can move the boat at very slowest of speeds between casts. He likes this because it gives him the opportunity to take two or three casts to likely looking spots while working a whole section of shoreline or is slowly moving from spot to spot through a creek.

Throughout this Southern area there is excellent bass fishing in the winters and this expert recalls the best single day of bass fishing he ever had. It was late in November and he took his limit of ten bass, which he has done often, but these fish, 6 weighed 5 to 6 pounds each while the other 4 weighed between 4 and 5 pounds—50 pounds of bass in one day. He likes this winter fishing and another advantage of it is that the fish are so tasty then. However, for the winter angler he suggests that good warm clothing is a must. One item Jimmy always uses in winter fishing is a "Float Coat." This is a warm coat that is also constructed to keep a person afloat if he should fall into the water. He recalls one January when another angler did fall in while they were running and the coat kept him afloat until he could be hauled out. That sold him on the value of this coat as a built in life preserver.

Jimmy is a professional newspaperman on Nashville's *Morning Tennessean,* one of the fine newspapers of the South. Here he doubles as a photographer and works in the sports section of the paper. He, of course, has tremendous interest in fishing and outdoors and several years ago joined the committee which produces Nashville's annual Outdoor Show. The profits from the show are donated to charities and Jimmy is rightfully proud of the fact that the show is now considered the finest outdoor show in the South, playing to big crowds and drawing a handsome profit annually.

Jimmy Holt is of the opinion that every major lake in the state holds some world's record fish in it and it is now up to Tennessee anglers to catch them and prove it to the world. He explains that every lake in the state is teeming with fish and there is always more than enough food for the fish while they also have the advantage of being able to feed all year long. His personal project is to get the new world record smallmouth—a 13 or 14 pounder. He knows where the big ones are, he knows what they will take, therefore, it is a problem of hooking into the fish. This he admits will take time, effort and lady luck, still he is confident. Good luck Jimmy.

3. MUSKELLUNGE FISHING WITH ARTHUR AND RUTH LAWTON

It is difficult to talk about the muskellunge fishing exploits of Arthur and Ruth Lawton without immediately breaking into the superlatives. This husband and wife fishing team have caught more big musky than any other people in the world. Mr. Lawton holds the world's record with a whopping 69 pound, 15 ounce monster, while Mrs. Lawton has taken the largest musky ever caught by a woman, a 68 pound, 5 ounce fish, only 1 pound, 10 ounces less than her husband's record fish. They have caught a half a dozen fish 60 pounds and over, plus over a dozen in the 50 pound category. This family conservatively estimates that they take a minimum of 60 musky a season weighing in excess of 20 pounds each.

The Lawton's regularly fish the Thousand Islands waters of the St. Lawrence River in the vicinity of Clayton, New York where they rent a fishing camp and store their boat. They travel to these waters from their home in Delmar, New York, a suburb of Albany, and make this 200 mile trip faithfully every weekend from the middle of May until they finally pull their boat out of the water in November.

Arthur Lawton has been fishing musky since 1936 when his brother, Gordon Lawton, introduced him to the sport. During these years of fishing he has developed his own very personalized style of musky fishing as well as his own theories of these fish. The first years of his musky fishing were in a large part experimental where he tried to apply the methods he had learned to capture Northern pike and walleyes to musky fishing. Here he went through the cycle of natural baits, cowbell spinners with huge bucktails, and finally came to plug fishing. It was about 1950 that Arthur Lawton decided that plug fishing was best for him and since that time he and his wife have fished plugs exclusively and as Mr. Lawton remarked, "Almost all of our fishing is done with Creek Chub Pikies which bring us our best luck."

During the early years of musky fishing when the Lawton's fished with natural baits, they would take a sucker 6 to 8 inches in length and string a wire hookup that Mr. Lawton had developed through the mouth of the fish and out through the fish's anus. Mr. Lawton, a refrigerator mechanic by trade, had developed a special hookup made from a wire that has the consistency of coat hanger wire. At his shop he twisted the wire so that at one end it was looped and could attach to the wire leader. The opposite end was formed into a snap to which he attached a set of double hooks. He rigged up by inserting the wire unit minus the hooks into the sucker's mouth and pushing it through the fish. Then he would attach the double 6/0 hooks to the fish holder and pull the shank of the hook back inside the baitfish, thus leaving the baitfish resting in the crook of the hook shanks. This left only the bend and barb of the hooks, one on each side of the fish, pointed up and poised for any attacking musky. This package was then weighted down and trolled through the musky haunts. Mr. Lawton feels this is still a good way to fish musky, but by experience he has found that he can catch more big fish through the use of plugs, thus he abandoned the natural baits.

Another method used extensively in the early days was the big 8/0, 9/0 or 10/0 cowbell spinners which a foot or two behind trailed a gigantic bucktail. The brush on these bucktails looks as big as shaving brushes and covers a 6/0 hook. Mr. and Mrs. Lawton remember the year that this combination was deadly, but later hits petered out while their luck increased with plugs, thus they also abandoned spinners. Arthur Lawton gives advice to anglers planning on using spinners when he says that those spinners that are copper on one side and silver on the other always seemed more attractive to the fish than the plain silver ones.

Mr. and Mrs. Lawton credit most of their big catches to plug fishing for it was after they switched that the records began coming. They use the various models of Creek Chub Pikies and Ruth Lawton favors the 6-inch lures while Arthur Lawton will stick strictly to the very large 8-inch ones. Mrs. Lawton likes the slightly smaller plugs because they make less drag on her line while Mr. Lawton fishes big ones as he is strictly after big fish and anything under 20 pounds doesn't interest him. Their method of fishing is to troll these plugs through the musky hotspots.

One of the points Mr. Lawton feels is very important to his success as a musky fisherman is the careful selection of his lures. As already explained, Arthur Lawton does almost all of his fishing with Creek Chub Pikie lures which he likes because they have a good motion in the water and because they are constructed with sturdy hooks that do not straighten out from the strain put on them by a big fish.

Arthur Lawton will inspect each plug he gets because he knows exactly what he expects of a plug. First he explains that even in the same make of plug there is often a difference in its motion. This may come about because the wood is balanced differently or because the hooks are placed in an ever so slightly different position, or because the hook eye is a fraction of an inch out of place or any number of other slight differences will make it act differently. Mr. Lawton tests each plug behind his boat while trolling to see how it moves through the water. He eliminates those that have no motion as well as those that are nervous and have too much motion. What he looks for is a plug that will swim in somewhat of a steady "S" as it is being trolled at a 4-mile per hour trolling speed. The slow "S" is the best action a plug can have as this is how a baitfish swims through the water. Time and time again it is the plugs that have this "S" motion that are the ones that have paid off for him.

Among the Creek Chub Pikies the Lawton's use both the single unit plug and the jointed plug interchangeably as they feel they both work equally well. Arthur Lawton emphasizes the import-ance of color in a plug for color makes a plug visible and at-tractive to a fish. One of his favorite designs is the original Pikie which is made up to look like a baitfish and is complete with a greenish-black fishlike striped back and a white belly. Fisherman Lawton has some of these original Pikies especially made up for him at the factory a half shade lighter than the regular com-mercial models. This slight difference helps to make this plug more natural looking and its lighter color makes it more visible to the fish. This Pikie is a fine lure all summer and fall and both Arthur and Ruth Lawton use it regularly. Early in the spring, when the musky season first opens the water may be somewhat muddy and then the brightly colored Rainbow Pikie, which is a highly visible lure, is very productive. A short while later as the water begins to clear they may switch to the Dace Scale Pikie, which is more subdued, but still brighter than most plugs.

One of the strange things angler Lawton has found is that at night the very dark plugs are the best producers. There was a time when he tried every brightly colored lure in his tackle box for night fishing, but he found that almost none of them were steady producers. Today he fishes the dark plugs such as the Black Scale Pikie or the Purple Eel Pikie and he gets excellent results. He does not know the reason for this apparent phenomenon, but from experience he does know that dark plugs take more musky at night than bright plugs.

One summer when the Lawton's took an extended musky fish-ing trip in the west they felt sure the Blue Flash Pikie would be a big producer. Much to his suprise his original Pikie far out-produced this and other selections. It seemed that the green waters of Northern Minnesota gave that Blue colored plug an unnatural look while the original Pikie looked like a perfect dinner to the musky and they lost no time hitting it. Again this proves another point Arthur Lawton makes and that is an angler must experiment until he finds a producer and sometimes one week may change a plug from the best producer to an unproductive lure. While fishing in good waters if the angler doesn't get any hits in a few hours it is time to change the lure.

Arthur Lawton has tried many kinds of plugs and quite regularly manufacturers send him plugs to try out. Recently he received a batch of European imports that have become very popular here. Mr. Lawton never did use these plugs because it was obvious the hooks were not constructed strong enough to hold a 30 pound musky let alone a 60 pound fish. For a time Mr. Lawton had some luck with a Homer La Blanc plug but he switched back to his favorite Creek Chub's again. Still on a recent trip to fish in a musky fishing contest at Eagle Lake Ontario he introduced some anglers there to this Homer plug and in the contest a fish caught on one of these plugs beat out Ruth Lawton's fish by a few ounces. The Homer plug produced very well in these waters.

The rig the Lawton's use for trolling their lures is to precede each plug with 4 feet of 25 to 30 pound test wire leader. In front of that they place a 4 or 6 ounce sinker which is torpedo shaped. This sinker is ringed on the end that is tied to the line while it has a snap on the end connecting to the leader. With this setup the line, sinker, leader and plug are in one continuing line, thus making the minimum amount of drag on the trolled package. This method of rigging also cuts down on snagging from other trolling setups. Then too, this terminal tackle can quickly be changed in case situations arise where additional weight may be needed or less weight is required. Here a second sinker can be put in place behind the original one, or in the reverse situation an extra sinker can easily be removed.

Their line is 100 yards of Ashway Nylon Bait Sport Casting and Trolling Line of 30 pound test. They like this particular line because the color changes every 10 yards, thus while trolling Mrs. Lawton might let out four 10 yard lengths while Mr. Lawton lets out only three 10 yard lengths. Then when one of them takes a fish they know that that is the correct length to let out, for it will have the lure traveling at just the right distance over the bottom. Generally, they like their lures to be about a foot or two off the bottom, right where a big fish sitting on the bottom will see it and smash into it.

The Lawton's fish hollow glass rods designed for light salt water fishing. They wanted a rod with plenty of strength to hold these big, fighting-mad fish and they needed a rod with the stiffness required to troll the big lures hour after hour. Their rods have a 5 foot tip and a two foot butt so that when they're on to a good musky they can drop the butt between their legs and get good leverage against the fish. The reel both of these fishermen prefer is a True Temper 922 standard reel which has a star drag built in and gives them all the strength they require of a reel.

A muskellunge generally hits with a smash, making the hookup very easy for the angler as the fish hooks itself. This begins the fight and immediately those rods really bend as the fish may rip off 30 to 40 yards of line on a run. Mr. Lawton remembers one particular big musky getting out in the channel and running right off the end of his line without ever getting a chance to turn him. Arthur Lawton warns that because muskies have hard boney mouths they are notorious hook spitters, as the hook can never really sink down deep into the flesh to grab a good hold. He says, "One of the times they can really get rid of a hook is when they come to the surface and start shaking their heads. The really big ones will get their body out of the water and begin shaking back and forth furiously, while small musky, about ten pounds, may start taking 10 foot leaps and sometimes spit the hook twice as far."

Arthur Lawton discovered one method that has helped to keep a fish on a hook. Mr. Lawton says, "I can tell when a fish is about to go skyward by that certain electric feeling in the line. When they're going up, I drop my rod tip right down to the water. This helps me to pull a jumping fish back to the water where he can more easily be fought." Ruth Lawton laughs, "Dropping the rod tip doesn't always work," she says, "I've seen those plugs fly 20 feet and more when they get rid of one."

Preparation for fighting a musky has to be made in advance of ever hooking one for the drag on the reel should be preset. They tighten the drag to the point where anyone stripping line from the reel by hand would feel the line cutting into their hand before the reel gives off any line. They estimate that they put close to 20 pounds of pressure on the drag. This heavy drag is dangerous and sometimes they get broken lines, but they do it because they want to put the fish against heavy pressure on every run it takes. This way the fish tires faster. They feel the most important thing in fighting is to always keep a tight line on the fish and to them that means the rods should always have a bend in them. Both Arthur and Ruth Lawton have adopted a method whereby they never pump a musky, but instead reel in at every opportunity when the fish is not running. Of course when a fish is going there is nothing anyone can do but to let him run, however the moment he stops it is back to work and reel. They always place their rod butt between their legs so as to get good leverage on the rod enabling them to put the most into their fight.

Arthur Lawton estimates that it takes about 1 hour of fighting to land a 60 pound musky—most smaller ones will take less time, although once it took an hour and a half to capture a fish half this size as it was hooked outside its mouth and under its jaw. If Mrs. Lawton has hooked the fish Arthur will slow the boat up and keep it moving along at just about idling speed. He will generally circle around the fish tying to keep the fish in the center of an imaginary circle. Sometimes while in the process of this circling maneuver he may edge the boat closer to the fish to steal some line.

When a fish is exhausted it can easily be led into the boat. Some fish will have swallowed water and air in the battle and may suddenly turn belly up before the end of the fight. The angler landing that fish should not fool himself into thinking that he has a dead fish because these tired, half-dead muskys can come to life very quickly as they are phenomenally tough fish with amazing lasting power.

Once the fish gets near the boat, Arthur Lawton will reach down and grab the handle of his 3-foot hand gaff. He then slips the hook of the gaff under the fish's jaw and in one motion inserts this hook into the soft fleshy meat under the fish's jaw. There is generally a spray and furious activity around the boat as he hauls the fishes head over the gunnel. Years ago Mr. Lawton would simply haul the fish right on deck, but he has learned that it pays to wait. Muskellunge have sharp canine teeth and they are strong fish so in a small boat they are dangerous shipmates. There was a time when some Wisconsin musky fishing guides would not pull a big one out of the water until they put some slugs from a revolver into the muskies head. To experienced sportsmen this extreme action isn't necessary for other methods of quieting them are successful.

What convinced Arthur Lawton not to bring them into the boat until anesthetized was the fish that lunged and dug its icepick teeth into his palm, opening a deep cut across his whole palm out to the end of his thumb. Another incident had a musky jumping and ripping Mr. Lawton's pants leg, but luckily missing any skin that time. These incidents were enough to convince him. Soon on every trip, along with the rods, reels and gaff, a regular hammer was added to the tackle box. Ever since, whenever a fishes head is brought over the side he reaches down and with the hammer gives the fish a few brisk smashes on the head. He hits the musky on a crown located on the fishes head right between the eyes and about 2 inches back on the head. He hits this crown with about the same strength that he would use to drive a nail into a board. "Hit this crown once or twice," says Arthur Lawton, "and the fish will quiver a few times and then will lie perfectly still like a real lady." They have had no trouble with even the biggest fish since this method of anesthesia became part of their fishing routine.

The Lawton's experience with musky is extensive and they

have learned many things about the fish. One of the interesting things they learned is how to keep many captured fish alive. When they are staying at camp for a week or more this insures that they have fresh fish to take back home with them. When a fish comes in, even when it is belly up, if Arthur Lawton wants to keep it, he will take it out of the water and hurry back to camp where he has a pen constructed in the water. Then before throwing the fish back in the water he will give the fish several hard slaps on its back. This in effect burps the fish and gets rid of all the air and water the fish has swallowed during the fight. After that the musky easily revives itself in the water and will live in that pen for days even without feeding. This way the Lawton's are always assured of bringing home absolutely fresh fish at the conclusion of every trip.

Arthur and Ruth Lawton's typical day of fishing is done from their own comfortable 17 foot fiberglass MFG boat which is complete with a cabin. Their boat is powered by a 50 hp Mercury outboard which they use to troll the 40 to 50 miles of water they will cover on each day of fishing.

Their regular fishing day begins about 9 A.M. Ruth Lawton says, "We used to start much earlier, sometimes as early as 3 A.M., but we found we didn't take any fish until later in the day so we now wait until after breakfast to start." Once in the boat they head upriver and troll all through a bay, only a short way from their cabin, spending possibly an hour working their lures along all the banks and ledges in the bay. When they are trolling they will constantly be searching for water 15 to 18 feet in depth. They have a depth finder aboard their boat, but in home waters they have combed the area so often that they seldom need the instrument and keep it along only for experimenting purposes. After working the bay they head out to an island and take three or four sweeps along the drop off at the island just at the section where the water is the desired 15 to 18 foot depth. Then they work another island close by and here again they work it with their usual 4 mph troll. After that it's rods up and a quick run to another spot located over 3 miles away off still another island. Some of their finest catches have been made here, therefore they are constantly on the alert for big hits in this area. Then they continue upriver for about 10 more miles before they swing over and start working the opposite shore, coming back down on the Canadian side. Here again they do their trolling along the islands at the drop offs and on the deep shoals.

Arthur and Ruth Lawton have won first place in the musky division of the *Field and Stream* Fishing Contest every year from 1956 through 1961. Ruth Lawton took top honors two years, in 1956 with a 60 pound, 8 ounce fish and in 1961 with a 68 pound, 5 ounce muskellunge. Arthur Lawton won from 1957 to 1960 inclusively with consecutive catches of 69 pounds, 15 ounces, 59 pounds, 5 ounces, 65 pounds, 13 ounces, and 61 pounds, 4 ounces. They have also won a contest for New York State fishermen, the Louis A. Wehle Fishing Contest, more times than anyone else. This fishing couple that was breaking world records and winning every fishing contest in sight quite naturally attracted considerable attention. One direct result was that a number of local boats began following them about. Mr. Lawton remembers one particular boat that followed them for years and eventually learned all the locations this couple had taken years to search out. The owner of that boat eventually died, but the next season the Lawton's were shocked to see that very same boat following them again. The boat had been sold to another owner who seemed to have inherited the sport of following the Lawtons. Mr. Lawton says, "Those people that followed us never had the success we had simply because they didn't understand this fishing and didn't fish in deep enough water. They thought they were following us, but I could see they were often a few yards off track and consequently were fishing in water that was too shallow. Small musky can be taken over the shallow shoals but the big fish will be down in 15 or more feet of water and will seldom come up higher." Sometimes during the summers Mr. and Mrs. Lawton will experiment and fish in water 30 to 40 feet in depth, but to date this has proved fruitless and invariably they head back to their regular spots. Arthur Lawton credits much of his fishing success to his ability to locate the right water to fish in.

After this angling couple complete the first 18 to 20 mile sweep of the river they come back to their cabin for lunch. Immediately after lunch it's out again this time first fishing the Canadian side in and around the famous 40 Acre Shoal off Gananoque. They continue trolling another 20 mile circle and coming back to their camp between 8 and 9 P.M.

During thousands of miles of trolling and thousands of muskellunge captures, these fishermen have found certain truths about these fish and this fishing. First they give no credence to the old rules that the angler must keep quiet for they keep a radio going in their boat constantly. There was a time when they maintained almost complete silence, but now they wouldn't care if an army choir from Camp Drum was 30 yards away singing, "Hail, Hail the Gang's all Here." Ruth Lawton says, "Making noise has no effect on the fish." Another point they long knew was sheer nonsense was the old belief that propellers scare the fish away from the boat. Mr. Lawton thinks that instead of scaring the fish they may well help to attract fish and he knows a few anglers who shine their propellers regularly. Another point they were happy to discover was nonsense was the belief that musky were caught only early in the morning and in the evenings. From their own experience they have found that their best catches have come right in the middle of the day. They feel there actually seems to be no general best time of day to fish for they have fished successfully all hours. They have begun days of fishing as early as 3 A.M. and at other times have fished well past midnight, but now for the most part they have given up these extreme hours generally restricting themselves to a fishing day that begins after sunup and continues until sunset. All their big fish were caught in this expanse of time.

There exists a persistent story that big musky over 40 or 50 pounds are blind, but the Lawton's are emphatic when they say this is pure nonsense. All the musky they have taken none were ever found to have defective eyesight. In fact, Mrs. Lawton says, "When you pull a big one up to the boat you should see the way it snaps at your hand if you place it too close—there is nothing wrong with their vision!"

However, there is one truism about musky which is very much a fact and that is that muskellunge suffer from sore mouths in the month of August. The fish lose their teeth then, therefore, for most anglers this is generally a lean month for musky. Arthur Lawton says, "When you take a musky in August you can immediately see their mouths are really hurting. Their teeth will be all loose and falling out while the new teeth that are ready to burst through the skin will have pus pockets on top of them—its obvious that the fish's mouth is giving him a lot of trouble."

Arthur Lawton adjusts his fishing in this month to compensate for the fishes' trouble. He learned that musky still hit during the month but they hit with only a fraction of their usual violence. This fisherman will lift his rod tip to strike his line at the feel of the slightest bump on the line. Often this may feel as lightly as if the lure just tripped some weeds but on many occasions the whole bottom exploded for the light touch was a 30 pound musky nudging the lure.

It was largely through the fishing efforts of Arthur and Ruth Lawton that the Thousand Islands Region of the St. Lawrence River is on the map as a leading musky fishing center. It was always known that there were musky here, but few of them were ever taken and even the local sportsmen were not aware of the superb musky fishing that was right at their doorstep. Fishermen by nature are quiet and never anxious to give their favorite locations away and for years Arthur and Ruth Lawton fished the area without anyone being aware of the fantastic catches they were getting. They fished alone and would store their fish in a huge refrigerator box and take the musky home to Albany without anyone seeing their catches. It wasn't until a guest of theirs showed some eye popping musky, a ½ dozen of them weighing 20 to 40 pounds each, to a local tackle store proprietor that word spread around about the gigantic fish that could be caught right here in the Clayton area. Others started fishing muskellunge and taking some, but never with the consistency and the size of the fish Mr. and Mrs. Lawton took. In some weeks of fall fishing, which they consider to be the best time, this family might take 10 to 20 musky totaling 300 to 500 pounds of fish. In one 9 day stretch they took 23 musky but could take home only 10 because their car couldn't carry any more fish in the trunk. Even this wasn't unusual for them but is remembered more because a reporter covered the trip than for the fish taken on it.

What really put the Thousand Islands on the fishing map was the day of September 22, 1957 when Arthur Lawton hit into his big one. He knew it was a good sized fish just from the way she dug down, but big ones were nothing new for him so within an hour he had the fish gaffed and aboard the boat. One thing Mr. Lawton does remember about this fish, "That big musky had just swallowed a Northern pike about as long as my arm and during the fight it spit the pike up. That pike remained on the line until just before the fish was landed when it finally fell off but if that fish would have kept that pike in him he would have weighed several pounds more." He didn't think to much of this big muskellunge and in fact never even weighed the fish until he had driven back to Albany. Here, to his amazement, the fish showed 69 pounds, 15 ounces and he knew he had beat out the Wisconsin fish of 69 pounds, 11 ounces which had been the standing record. Immediately after that the Associated Press and other news services printed stories of the capture while sporting magazines did articles of the event and reams of publicity were printed on the quality of the St. Lawrence muskellunge fishing.

Mr. and Mrs. Arthur Lawton were now the most famous musky fishing couple in the land and a dinner was held in their honor by the Gananoque Chamber of Commerce for they had taken the fish on the 40 Acre Shoal. But fame brought headaches too for it was soon after that boats started following them. They adjusted to that too, but it is still annoying for them to come to one of their favorite out-of-the-way spots only to find someone that may have been following them the week before is already fishing there.

Arthur Lawton has a word of advice for prospective musky anglers and that is that musky fishing takes patience. Ruth Lawton adds, "Plenty of patience!" He advises that this is specialized fishing where the angler should be prepared for long periods of experimenting and waiting. His advice is that if the angler is to do his fishing in the St. Lawrence or one of the big lakes he should immediately begin by fishing plugs. He also feels that guides can help someone in new waters, but any waters an angler intends to make his home waters should to a great extent be explored individually. Much of the thrill of fishing comes from finding your own hot spot.

To Mr. Lawton what happens after an angler gets some fish is most important in the making of a musky angler. "The angler must always mark the spot and take careful and accurate land sightings so that he can come back to the exact place again, for the chances are if one musky is taken in a place it will hold more fish." He goes on to explain an experiment that was recently conducted in Wisconsin where some small musky were caught and then sped a mile or more away from that location. Each musky was then tagged by tying a balloon on a string to the fish after which the fish were released. The anglers were able to follow the fish by watching the balloon move across the water. The strange thing was that these musky headed back to the same spots where they were caught. Of course it is premature to draw final conclusions, but it did indicate a homing tendency of the fish. It also helps explain why fish will be taken in exactly the same spots year after year.

Mr. Lawton also feels that musky have definite migratory tendencies, moving up and down river during spawning as well as moving into very deep water and then coming on the banks with changing water conditions. Because the musky will return to the same spots time after time Mr. Lawton stresses the importance of learning to find the musky hot spots. Recently when the St. Lawrence was dredged it changed some of his holes and in some instances he had to search out new places because of the change in the water bottom. "Musky fishing," he says, "is patience and experimenting and always looking for new hot spots while carefully remembering the exact location of old ones."

Arthur Lawton feels an angler does best fishing waters where he will be able to spend time to locate his own good spots. Generally this means fishing in musky waters nearest the anglers home and depending on where the angler lived it could be any of the following productive waters: The St. Lawrence River, The Niagara River, Lake St. Clair, Chippewa Lake, Lake of the Woods, Eagle Lake, or any other known musky water. He feels if it has musky and it is a place where the angler can fish and study the water it will be a good spot for him to do his fishing. As for where the biggest musky may be, Mr. Lawton feels they may be in the waters of the Lake of the Woods or Eagle Lake, Ontario for these waters seem perfectly suited for musky propagation. He feels these two lakes are more suitable for growing huge musky than even the St. Lawrence River.

The musky is a fish that is native only to the cold waters of the North American continent. It is the largest freshwater member of the pike family of fish and it has really inspired the imagination of people as to their maximum size. Some stories insist they go to 500 pounds and over ten feet in length. How big do musky go? The males are rather puny reaching a maximum size of 40 inches and about 25 pounds in weight while the females are the giant of the species. Art Lawton feels that the fish may well go to 150 pounds. There have been some netted in Lake of the Woods over 100 pounds in weight and Chippewa Lake Wisconsin gave up a 102 pounder to the netters. Other records all indicate that the fish go well over the century mark.

It may seem strange coming from the angler who has caught more big musky than any man alive as well as the world record fish, but Mr. Lawton still says, "Some day, if I live long enough, I'm going to catch a big fish!"

4. STEELHEAD AND SALMO NFISHING WTH DALE IVIE

Mr. Dale Ivie fishes the streams of Oregon and Washington almost daily and he considers them to be the world's finest steelhead and salmon waters. He has fished constantly for 20 years and in that time has averaged 200 steelhead and 100 salmon annually.

Mr. Ivie lives at Vancouver, Washington, with his wife and three children. A gunsmith by profession, he makes some of the finest custom gun stocks in the West Coast. His love is steelhead and salmon fishing and he has fished them in the ocean, in the big Columbia, and in other major rivers, but his favorite fishing is to get on a medium sized Columbia feeder stream such as the Cowlitz River, The Clakamas, or the Toutle River, find a hole and go to work.

One of his favorite streams is the Lewis River of Washington where he knows almost every hole on the stream from having fished it so often. He says, "The steelhead come into these streams to breed; therefore, they will generally be on the move to reach the small feeding streams at the headwaters. However, the fish are generally not in a hurry to get there, so they will move into the streams that we fish and will stay. Then, depending on the conditions, they may stay in a hole a few minutes or a month before they move up to the next spot. As one group of fish move out of one hole another group may move into it following the same general procedure. Sometimes when an angler fishes one hole for several hours he may find the steelhead have suddenly moved out, while at other times an empty hole may suddenly fill up. Part of this great sport is being able to locate the holes where the fish are staying."

Steelhead anglers pride themselves on being able to find holes with fish. Dale Ivie says, "I will often come to a hole and I might not even fish it, or I will take only one or two casts because I know it just doesn't hold fish. At times I wear polarized sun glasses to help me look into the water and occasionally I can see a flash of a fish turning, but it is more a sixth sense you get with experience. The water and weather conditions have much to do with it for when the water level is high and the stream is off colored, the fish will tend to stay in only the deepest holes or in places where they are protected from the rushing currents. When the water gets low and clean, the fish will stay in shallow holes and I fish here. I recall once going to the White Salmon River and from the water conditions I knew exactly where I wanted to fish. Two other anglers were already there and they were just about ready to move on because they hadn't caught anything, but I got that feeling. On the very first cast I let my bait go deep into the hole and wacko! I hooked and caught a beautiful 10 pounder. This has happened quite often.

On an other occasion a famous lady angler and casting champion came to Portland. She had gone out for 4 days and hadn't caught a thing and on her fifth day here she came out with me. I had fished regularly during the week and knew the water conditions so I immediately thought of a hole on the Kalama that should have holding fish. On my first cast I hooked a 10 pounder and landed it. Then with a few minutes of explanation, which was all she needed as she really knew the sport, she was fishing. After a short time she hooked her first steelhead and battled it in. A 16 pounder and was she proud."

The time the fish stay in a hole varies—it may be only a few minutes for a fish to get a little rest and gather energy to go crashing against the rapids, moving further upstream. Other fish will stay in a hole for a day while some will remain there a week or more before they too move on upstream.

Mr. Ivie explains that catching the fish that are on the move is difficult and it is really only luck when you get one because you just never know where they are. Anglers generally forget about the moving fish and instead concentrate their efforts on the fish that will be in a hole for a length of time.

When steelhead are staying they get down on the bottom where the water is not rushing hard. An angler moves along the bank until he comes to a hole and then fishes it. Mr. Ivie says, "I generally like to fish a hole completely from one end to the other. I start at the head of the hole and throw my bait out letting it hit the water and sink down and begin to drift downstream. I let the bait drift as far as I can, then I retrieve and cast again working the same general area. Gradually I will work the front of the hole first, then the middle and finally the tail-out. It is from the middle back to the tail-out that most fish will be caught. And the biggest steelhead will usually be taken way back in the tail-out just before the rapids. I always make sure that my bait goes right back into the rapids because in turbulent Western streams often there appears fast ripples on top but a few feet under the water may be moving slowly. There are several holes I know where the surface water is actually white yet 12 feet down the water is nearly still. This is often excellent water for the lunkers and when I find it I really work it over. I caught my biggest steelhead, a wooping 25 pounder, which I later released, in the East fork of the Lewis River way back in water that was white on the surface."

Dale Ivie feels one of the most important things all prospective steelhead anglers should learn about is the fish and their habits of life. The steelhead are, of course, the famous sea run rainbow trout of the West Coast. These fish are in all the major rivers North of San Francisco all the way up to Alaska. Steelhead will leave the ocean for freshwater in all months of the year but those of the fall and winter are the big mature ones. The fish entering during the late spring and summer are immature but they will mature while in freshwater. Generally those fish which have exceedingly long trips to their breeding grounds enter as late spring and summer immature fish. All the fish going above Bonneville Dam are summer and spring fish which will stay in the stream until the following winter when they will mature and breed. Those fish which enter freshwater in the fall and winter are mature fish that will head right up to the spawning water. The big, strong, fully-grown, silvery, mature steelhead winter fish constitute a large number of fish in the Columbia and other major downstream tributaries.

Steelhead are born in freshwater as baby rainbow trout and they remain in freshwater streams for approximately two years. While immature fish, they feed on algae and whatever small food particles that can be found. At the end of two years the young trout will be 6 to 8 inches long and then start downstream. They go downstream pushed by the flood water riding the currents to the ocean. It is only where dams are built without proper fish ways that the fish don't get out to sea which is the natural instinct. Those fish remain in freshwater as rainbow trout but never attain the size or have the fight of the ocean run fish.

Once out in the ocean they quickly learn to feed on other fish and they grow physically. They are great travelers and roam over much of the Northern Pacific. Tagged fish from Oregon have been captured in the Gulf of Alaska some thousands of miles out in ocean, while others were tagged in the ocean and later recaptured back in Oregon. These fish tend to stay far out at sea and remain in the cold Northern ocean thus protecting themselves. A few fish fall prey to other fish, but by and large the time steelhead spend in the ocean is a relatively safe period for them.

After one year a few of the fish will return to their freshwater birthplace. Like the salmon they return to where they were born, and these first year fish will now be from 3 to 6 pounds in weight. However, most steelhead stay a second year in salt water and then come back fully mature fish weighing from 8 to 10 pounds depending on how well they had fed in the ocean.

The mature steelhead return to the rivers of Alaska, British Columbia, Washington, Oregon and the Northern part of California depending on their heredity. They are vigorous and strong fish and some of them will run hundreds of miles upstream in some of the fastest rivers in the world. Steelhead once swam up the Columbia into Idaho and the Snake River going upstream for over 500 miles. Lately portions of the Snake River have been cut off by dams without fish ladders, but it is still a majestic trip.

What is more amazing is that the fish make these trips and have enough strength left to breed and return to saltwater to fatten up for another year. The steelhead in from the sea do not feed in freshwater and some have been kept a year in hatcheries without feeding and apparently not hurting the fish. An ichthyologist can tell from the fish's scales just how many trips it made to the ocean and one particular specimen was thought to have made as many as seven trips. Most fish will make two trips, with three not at all unusual.

Mr. Ivie says, "It is those second run fish that we want to hit into. They come back weighing 15 to 25 pounds, strong and mean as a finely trained prizefighter. Hit into one of these and you are in for some sport that cannot be surpassed.

"On the Columbia we have fish that come in from the sea in every month during the winter. There will be a run in December, January, February, March and another one in April. These fish are bright silvery in color and lively as a March hare. The winter fish are coming in to breed and they are the sportiest. During the later spring, summer and fall the steelhead that come in are the immatures as they mature in freshwater 6 to 8 months later. Those fish going many miles upstream breed the following winter.

"Although the steelhead in from the ocean do not feed during the time they are in freshwater it is not difficult to get them to take a hook," says Dale. "They take certain things or attack objects and it is on these instincts that we fishermen build our fishing methods."

The most productive method of fishing developed for steelhead is a relatively simple one of fishing a cluster of salmon eggs along the bottom of a stream. This is especially good for the winter fish and Mr. Ivey readily admits he caught most of his 20 pounders using this method. He says, "During a fishing season I buy between 100 and 150 pounds of salmon eggs from the salmon canneries. I make sure I get big ripe eggs that are about the size of pearls on a lady's necklace. These will be eggs that are only 2 or 3 weeks away from spawning. I then pack them in borax as this preserves and hardens the eggs and membranes holding the eggs together. I keep them in a freezer at home.

"When I go out fishing I take a days supply which is about as many as fit into a one pound coffee can. I find the best way to fish eggs is in clusters, because I think, the clusters are more visible in the water and are more likely to draw hits than single eggs. Some anglers fish single eggs on very small hooks because they have trouble holding clusters on a hook. I know some anglers who put the eggs in sacks of hair like material and place this on a hook. However, today most of us who preserve our eggs in borax find this toughens the membranes so that the eggs hold together as a cluster."

The way Mr. Ivie prepares his hook is another innovation that helps hold the eggs to the hook. He ties the mono-filament line directly on the hook in a unique way by first passing the line through the eye of the hook and then over the hook shank. On the shank he takes several turns of the line and then tying the line to the shank. He then places the egg cluster of 8 to 10 eggs on the hook and pushes the line through the eye of the hook making a loop. The eggs are placed inside the loop and the line is tightened holding the eggs.

"To anyone not a steelhead or salmon angler, it must seem strange indeed that fishermen use bait on fish that are not feeding." Mr. Ivie explains, "These fish have an instinct to take eggs.

When the fish are breeding, and this is even more apparent with salmon than steelhead, after the female has laid its eggs and has a male milt them, she drops back behind the nest and any eggs that are washed out of it she pounces on them to destroy the eggs. This is nature's way of taking care of the species, for what happens is that sterile eggs or improperly formed eggs are lighter in weight than ripe healthy eggs thus these eggs are destroyed by the fish."

He explains, "The fish live on instinct all their lives. They have the instinct to come back after traveling thousands of miles at sea and return to the stream of their birth—they have the instinct to know just when this should be done and they have the instinct to destroy eggs in the water.

"A steelhead is not a difficult fish to get to take a hook. The important thing is to get the bait down deep and in front of the fish. If you don't get the bait down, you don't catch fish—it is as simple as that.

"When a fish takes the hook I can almost always feel the slight bump on the line, but I still get fooled on occasions with the sinker bouncing along the bottom. Other times the steelhead will just suck the eggs in and you can't feel a thing. When I do feel a hit I simply lift my rod-tip and tighten the line. The fish have very soft mouths and it takes almost no pressure to insert the hook—in fact many fish hook themselves.

"Once the line is tightened on a steelhead—look out—they explode! I have had them come up and do 20 jumps running from one end of a pool to another. They will run in any and every direction. Sometimes they come straight at me or they may run upstream away from me heading right into the rapids. Some fish will fight on for an hour or more, but some quit after only 10 minutes. One thing I am convinced of is that an angler does not tire a steelhead, but he catches it by breaking the fishes spirit. Take a fish that quits fighting easily it may suddenly burst back to life just before it is landed and fight on for ½ hour more. If you want a fish, let him know you are the boss and then you have that fish captured.

"One of the real dangers when fighting a fish is when it suddenly turns and gets into fast water heading downstream. I have followed fish a ¼ mile stumbling along the shore or wading trying to keep up with them. It is exciting, but it is too easy to lose a fish this way. In the fast moving western streams the fish use their strength and the pressure of the moving water to strain the line and rip the hook from their mouths. The angler must do everything he can to stop the fish from heading into the rapids. One trick I found that works very well on a fish definitely heading there is to simply put the reel on free spool and give the fish all the slack line in the world. This will momentarily surprise him. Often he stops running and turns around facing upstream which is his natural position.

"When a fish does get into the rapids, and they do, you are in for some fireworks. The steelhead will move along that water so fast, line will rip off with such velocity you'll wish you had 1,000 yards of it. I have had them take 100 yards of line in less than 10 seconds. Sometimes even when they are in fast water I try the free spool trick and occasionally it works. Generally though I have to scurry after them the best I can. When I fish I have a minimum of 150 yards of line of either 8 or 12 pound monofilament so I have enough line for a good run. I try like all get out to stop a fish from getting into fast water but those that do certainly make for some bristling moments in this sport and they are the ones you are proudest of—if you hold them."

The fishing can get acrobatic and Dale Ivie wears chest-high waders. On top of them he puts on a pair of old cotton pants as there are many briar bushes along the streams and the pants help prevent the waders from ripping. On the soles of his boots to stop from slipping he has added nylon carpet. This is the same material that nylon swimming pool mats are made of and it works superbly. Previously he had used felt for extra gripping, but the nylon had as much grip and lasted much longer.

His choice of tackle for stream fishing is a 10 foot fast taper salmon fly rod. Sometimes he will switch to an 8½ foot fly rod of the same fast tip action, but today even when fishing his fly rod he will put a closed face spinning reel on it. He then uses this combination the same way he would his regular spinning outfit. Mr. Ivie now does his fishing alternately with 8 and 12 pound test monofilament line—making sure he has at least 150 yards of line on the reel. He explains that in high water he likes the heavier test line because he can control it better while during the summers, and fall when the water is lower he will go for the lighter line as it is more deceptive.

Mr. Ivie has made certain tackle innovations and one is that he fishes his closed faced reel with an adapter on the rod so that the reel is cranked with his left hand. To get the reel in this position there is currently an adapter that can be purchased, but originally he made his first one in a machine shop. With this arrangement he presses the button of the reel when he wants to cast, and with his forefinger grabs the line just as he would if he were casting an open faced reel. Then he lets fly. The instant the line hits the water he is ready to retrieve and no hand changing of the rod is required.

Dale Ivie likes to dream up new tackle devices and one of his rods that he made the entire reel seat is enclosed in wrap around cork. This is his personal cold weather rod, for on a stream with snow and ice it is much easier holding cork than metal.

His terminal rig for egg fishing consists of a 2/0 Mustad hook, pattern 92550, and a strip of lead for a sinker. Generally about a foot above the hook he ties an auxiliary line possibly 6 inches long. This is a separate sinker line. Some anglers use line of a slightly lighter test than what they are fishing so that when a snag occurs it is this auxiliary line that breaks and they lose only a sinker. Much terminal tackle is lost in steelhead and salmon fishing, and Dale Ivie keeps long strips of lead with him. When he needs another weight he simply takes out his long nosed plyers and snips off a ¼ inch piece and then with the plyers squeezes the lead on the short leader line. Generally about ¼ ounce will take the hook to the bottom and will be light enough to allow the bait to keep moving along the bottom. To be effective a bait must move along the bottom so that it drifts to the fish.

Snags are unavoidable in this kind of fishing. In an effort to cut them down Dale Ivie feels that if the angler tries to fish slightly ahead of where his hook and sinker is it will help as it will keep the hook moving ever so slightly above the bottom, bouncing instead of dragging the bottom. Still snags occur and when they happen he just drops the rod-tip pointing it directly at the spot the hook snagged and then he walks the rod away from the spot. If the angler is lucky the tackle will free itself, if he is half lucky the lead leader will break, and if it is a real snag the line will break. Thirty snags in a day of fishing are not uncommon. He says, "There are no better hook changers than steelhead anglers."

When Dale Ivie started fishing over 20 years ago, basket fishing was the accepted method. Here the angler gets a fly rod and uses an oversized fly reel with 150 yards of line and backing. Then tied around the anglers waist is a basket. The angler got ready to cast by stripping line from the reel and dropping it in the basket in a circular shape. When he cast his bait the line that had been carefully placed in the basket rushes out through the rod guides. This gives the angler a friction free cast which allowed him to cast to the same places that today's spinning rods reach. This method was more difficult to master than spinning but the experts of the Northwest had excellent results and there still is a small group of basket fishermen. Dale Ivie thinks the new equipment is so much less cumbersome that it warranted the change to spinning tackle.

Dedicated sportsmen such as Dale Ivie, who fish for sport and enjoyment, are all conservation conscious. With Mr. Ivie, conservation begins with himself as he feels if he doesn't follow good practices how can he expect others to follow them. Mr. Ivie explains that often the problem is not how to catch steelhead, but how to safely release them. He keeps a towel clip on his lapel. This is a medical clamp used in operations to firmly hold a towel. When the clip is closed down on a fish the hooklike points are inserted into the fish directly under the dorsal fin and the pincers lock. If the fish is a keeper he is landed this way. The two prongs enter the fish behind the dorsal, and do not actually hurt the fish. Mr. Ivie explains it this way, "A fish in rough water is always scraping against abrasive rocks and through centuries it has built tolerance to cuts and rips in its skin." Then he points out, "Breaks in the skin do not cause a fish to bleed and proof of this is that tagged fish live for years. The clips I use inflict the same type of small punture in the fishes skin as some tagging does."

Mr. Ivie says, "I started using the clips so that I could release a fish safely. In the course of a year, I will catch between 200 and 250 steelhead, and in Washington I'm permitted to keep only 25 fish a year. My problem has been largely being able to release the fish safely. With the clip I never physically touch my fish as I put the clamp on the fish, then I simply reach down and cut the line leaving the hook in the fishes mouth. I then unhinge the towel clip and the fish is free to swim off. If no one else captures that fish it will breed and return to salt water and come back to the stream again a year later. The hook left in the fish's mouth will from the internal acids of the fish and from the water disintegrate within a few days. I have caught fish with hooks in them and the hooks in no way hurt the fish.

"What will hurt the fish is trying to remove a hook from a steelheads mouth. Trout anglers biggest complaint against bait fishermen is they kill every fish they hook. Luckily steelhead and salmon caught on eggs are not hooked deeply as the fish only sucks in the eggs to crush them and spit them out again.

"The thing that really has to be watched is bleeding because a fish that bleeds is a dead fish. Fish have cold blood and there is nothing in their system to allow blood to congeal, therefore, if the hook makes any kind of wound in the gills, that fish will bleed to death. Usually a barbed hook sunk deep in a fishes gills when removed will make that fish bleed and will consequently kill the fish. It is far safer to simply cut the line and let nature disintegrate the hook—it won't take long and it doesn't bother the fish.

"Another danger for killing a fish comes from bodily handling it. This is why I stopped using landing nets for you are much more apt to handle the fish in the net. I try not to touch the fish at all, however on occasions when I do I make certain my hands are in water during any handling. The handling of a fish with human hands often causes a fish to get a fungus that later kills the fish. We in fishing are fortunate because we can fully enjoy the sport of catching a fish and we can still release it and let it live on, the only requirement is that we are careful."

As Mr. Ivie releases many of the steelhead he catches he has tried such things as barbless hook fishing. He says, "When I'm fishing and I don't intend to keep the fish I will pull out my plyers and give the barb on my 2/0 Mustad hook a squeeze. The barb will fold right back making it an almost perfect barbless hook. Now if you hook into a 15 pounder you are in for some excitement as you can never relax the line. There is no margin for slack as the hook slips out too easily and this means a tight line on the fish at all times. The strangest thing is that I find I still hate to lose a fish, release them yes, but lose them in a fight no. I find myself trying even harder to make sure I land the steelhead. I have had fish on that took over twenty jumps trying all the time to spit the hook, but by keeping the line tight I held many of them. Fish will tear into the rapids and I've lost many of them, but I've kept my fair share too. It is quite a feeling trying to hurry after a fish that just took 50 yards of line when you know if he gets slack he will almost certainly be able to get rid of the hook. Sometimes I've hit a fish just in from the sea, wild as a bronco and strong as one, and I was wondering just what I was trying to do. This develops into a real contest of the fisherman's skill against the fish, and he who makes the mistake loses. It is quite a challenge."

The individual challenge of angler against fish often becomes intriguing. Mr. Ivie explains that often he will be fishing a hole and may get a very light hit several times. After this has happened a number of times, the angler knows there is only one fish in the hole and it is striking very gently at the offering. Here is the challenge—one fish against one angler, with the fish having the advantage of being in its own element. Often he will bait up and then spend several hours trying for that fish knowing full well that if he moved to another hole he would in all probability increase his catch.

When the angler is dueling one fish the angler must really sharpen his skills. He must keep his line taut and ready to strike at the first sign and he will spar with the fish for hours. Dale feels that when you hook that fish you really feel the satisfaction of accomplishment but he warns that many of these individual duels will be won by the fish, as the angler simply will not be able to hook the fish.

Steelhead males, unlike many other fish including salmon, will be the biggest fish of the specie. Almost all the big steelhead are males, as the females simply do not grow as large. Mr. Ivie also states the males are the best fighters. He says, "A male fish is more active. It jumps more and has more fury in its runs and seems to fight longer too. The male can easily be identified by its large unproportioned mouth and big jaws while the female has a much smaller mouth. I can often tell the sex while the fish is on the line by the fight."

In every season except the winter season, other methods of fishing are used quite extensively. One method that is gaining popularity fast is fly fishing for steelhead. It has actually been done a long time, but there are certain innovations added that make it more popular with the local sportsmen, many of whom earlier shunned fly fishing.

Angler Dale Ivie explains that during the winter there are few, if any, anglers who fly fish. It is not so much that the fish won't take the flies, but it is more they are impractical to use. The fish are right on the bottom and with the high fast running cold water it is much better using salmon eggs as they can sink down much easier.

In the lower Columbia and its tributaries there are some steelhead all year long and it presents the anglers with many varied seasonal water conditions for catching fish. He says, "I really enjoy fly fishing and it is getting more popular all the time among the sports anglers. But still I restrict my fly fishing to anytime the water level gets low.

The western streams always have a good flow so the angler has two problems in fly fishing. One is getting the fly down deep enough to the fish, and the other is getting the fly out into the current where the fish will be found. They have both been solved for anglers with the advent of the shooting-head line.

The shooting-head line is a tapered weighted line that is approximately 30 feet in length with loops at both ends. The regular monofilament line from the reel is attached to one end of the line while 3 or 4 feet of leader to the fly is attached at the other end. The advantage is that the line shoots out from the reel and then sinks once it hits the water taking the fly down with it. It solved both problems of getting the line out into the middle of the stream and taking the fly down below the surface since it is a weighted line.

Shooting-head lines came onto the steelhead fishing sport about the same time that spinning was getting popular. It was developed by the Golden Gate Casting Club and originally was used on the Klamath, where it really popularized fly fishing on that stream. Fly fishing utilizing shooting-head lines spread all over the West coast and it is the basic line for steelhead fly fishing.

"The flies we use out West would make an Eastern dry fly trout angler feel like he was having a nightmare." says Mr. Ivie. "We use large gaudy colored flies and one of my favorites is a Chartreuse Green Fly. This is excellent in water near the ocean. I believe the fly represents a small plant life and the steelhead strike it. A few of my friends have good results with the Brown Hackle Fly and I've taken fish on the Bucktail Streamer. Other patterns include the Surveyor, Edison Tiger, Cummings and the Capra Streamer are among the many that produce."

When the water level recedes and when the water gets warmer the fish become more active, making it better for fly fishing. Steelhead never come near the top for any length of time and they are always fished under the surface, however, it isn't always necessary to get right to the bottom the way anglers do with the salmon eggs. A fly has to be fished wet and generally the deeper it runs the better it is, but some fish will be taken just under the surface. Mr. Ivie feels that the biggest fish are not taken on flies, but a 6 to 10 pounder on flies is not at all uncommon. He feels that if flies were used more in the cold weather when the real big fish are in, it would produce the big fish, but since egg fishing is so much better they take the big ones. The flies just don't sink as fast as the eggs and sinker combination therefore in fast water the natural bait is generally preferred by the best sports anglers.

A fly is cast out and given time to sink. Then it is permitted to drift down into the pools. Mr. Ivie gives no specific instructions for striking a fish on a hit, for unlike the trout the steelhead will hit slow and deliberate. The fish does not spit the fly out the way a trout will and most fish simply hook themselves, in fact he feels the angler that strikes his line will in most cases pull the fly away from the fish. The angler has only to tighten up the line on a hit and get ready for the big battle ahead. In low water the fish will often skip across the water in 10 to 20 leaps and the fight will be spectacular.

Mr. Ivie says, "Fly fishing is growing rapidly. It is great fishing and there is no doubt that taking a fish on a fly does add satisfaction to one's day."

When the steelhead are in the stream during low water they tend to become spooky and the angler is hard pressed to get them to take any offering. I was told by one old steelhead angler of one bait that really takes the fish and when he said it, I thought he was kidding—dandelion buds. Place a small one on a hook and drift it through a pool and sometimes it works better than I care to admit. Other strange baits that get the fish to hit include rose buds or buds of almost any flower. Fish will take night crawlers or anything that wiggles, swims or makes a motion. What the steelhead do is attack any foreign object in the water. A bud is something strange moving through the water and the same is true of a worm busily wiggling away—if it is strange to the stream it may well bring a hit and it generally works best during summers in low water.

One other popular kind of sports fishing for steelhead is bank fishing on the Columbia or near the mouth of one of the big tributaries. Dale doesn't bank fish too often, but everytime he does it he enjoys it. Here the angler gets along the bank of the big river and casts 150 to 175 feet into the river and lets the lure and baits sink. He then sits down and enjoys the country while he waits for action.

Dale Ivie feels this is highly recommended fishing for anyone feeling blue, as bank fishermen generally cluster together at the various hot spots along the river. When there is a good run of steelhead or salmon on the river it is often hard to find a parking spot near one of the better known spots. One of the nice things of being on the bank is mixing conversation with men who appreciate this beautiful country and really enjoy fishing.

All kinds of gear will turn up on the river, but Dale Ivie prefers a 10 foot casting rod of somewhat sturdy construction and made for two handed casting. Line here should be 20 to 30 pound test monofilament. The terminal tackle is often arranged with a 3-way swivel—one holding the line, one, a 12 to 18 inch line of 10 to 12 pound test connecting to the sinker which will vary from 4 to 10 ounces, and the third line connecting to the hook or lure being used.

The fishing is generally done on the lee side of a sandbar or behind some point where the flow of water is broken and it affords the fish a good resting spot. Anglers will cast their lines out so they sit on the bottom until the fish see them. Many anglers place a spinner of some kind in front of their bait as the flash helps attract attention of the fish. Some anglers use salmon eggs as baits, but the imitations are taking over. One used quite regularly is the Oakie Drifter, which is a plastic cluster of eggs. Others used regularly are the Spinning Glow and Flatfish.

There is only one real rule of bank fishing and that is to have the line hold bottom and not drift across and tangle other anglers lines. Bank anglers have no patience with people who tangle lines because it means work and time away from the pleasures of fishing. However, once a fish is hit the angler who has the fish on gets the right of way over everyone. Other anglers reel in when they may be in the way. The catches from the bank are good for both steelhead and salmon when the big runs are in the river.

Mr. Ivie says, "I have fished for steelhead all over Oregon, Washington, Idaho and in parts of British Columbia and these are great sportsfish. It does not matter whether one gets the fish in the famous Rogue River, the Umpqua, the Snake, Cowlitz, the Fraser River, or any of the thousands of rivers and streams in this vast area as these are purebred sportsfish that always create excitement for the angler."

* * *

There is one other fish in the Northwest that stirs the hearts and souls of anglers and that is the mighty king salmon. The king salmon of course has more names than appear in the social register and a few of them include chinook, spring salmon, tyee, tule and quinnat. King salmon or chinook are the most common and any reference to king is rightly so as fish taken have gone over 100 pounds. The biggest ever taken on rod and reel was 92 pounds and it came from the Skeena River in British Columbia back in 1959.

The Western chinook fishing fraternity consists of the same group of anglers who are the steelhead regulars therefore many of the upstream fishing methods are very similar for both fish. There are many anglers who use their same tackle for both species. Mr. Ivie says, "I use a 10 foot rod for salmon which is slightly sturdier than my steelhead rod and I like my salmon rod to be medium action because the fish are bigger and the extra body in the rod helps." The hooks and sinker setup is exactly the same as with steelhead.

On the Columbia the king salmon runs begin in February with the fish entering the mouth of the river. Some move upstream rapidly while others stay in the lower bay water and offshore water for considerable periods of time before they begin moving. Schools of fish enter the river in March and April and progressively more fish come in every week through these months. The runs will reach their peak during April, but there will be good salmon runs in May and June and in fact there will be chinooks here right through July in some years. Of course, like all fishing, certain aspects of the runs are entirely unpredictable because in some years, right in the middle of a good season, there may suddenly appear a void where no fish enter these waters for 2 and sometimes even 3 weeks at a time.

He explains, "Again we are able to catch the fish by styling our fishing methods so that it tempts the salmon's instinct to strike at certain things. It may seem strange catching fish averaging 20 pounds and exceeding 50 pounds at times on a 6 or 8 salmon egg cluster that weighs no more than 1/4 of an ounce, but this is what we do. In fact, during the summers, when the water is low and there are kings about we fish with only 2 or 3 eggs in a cluster as this is ample."

Dale explains that in salmon fishing it is again the primary concern of the angler to find water where there are fish staying. He says, "I once was fishing on the Nestucka River and I came to a pool where I just felt there were some fish. There were already several other anglers around the pool and they weren't catching anything, but I had that distinct feeling as the water looked deep and heavy—it was perfect looking salmon water. The spot I wanted on the hole had no anglers so I took up my position. I was using my regular spinning outfit and 6 pound test line. I cast out so that my sinker and eggs would drop right to the bottom of the very deepest part of this pool. On my third cast my line went tight and at first I actually thought that I had snagged bottom, but then the bottom started to move and I knew I had hooked a good one.

"That fish shook its head back and forth and moved through the water hard and deliberately, the way a big chinook will. I gave him line when he wanted it but I continued putting pressure on him. Over the period of a half an hour I managed to work him in and I was very careful as I was well aware of the fact I was fishing with 12 pound line. Finally I got him into shallow water and, wow, what a fish, but he took off again shaking angrily and diving for deep water. My rod bent, but I worked another 15 minutes and finally brought the fish in so that I could insert the towel clip behind its dorsal fin. I dragged the king up on the bank and it turned out to be the biggest salmon I ever took—a 47 pound monster.

"I went back to fishing and within 15 minutes had another strike. This one turned out to be a 43 pounder. The two fish taken from that stream weighed in at 90 pounds—quite a day. Again I want to point out two reasons for catching them. First, as I had suspected, there were holding fish in the hole and in spite of the fact I was the fourth angler at the hole, I had the best spot because my bait was able to get down into the deepest section of the hole which was right in front of the fish."

Mr. Ivie points out that his fishing is basic fishing as he has no secret lures or baits to offer as sure fire advice for taking fish. Yet, he explains that he never really had a bad salmon year for the last 10 years, as every year he has taken at least 100 kings. He points out the important thing is to find the holes where the fish are staying and then find the exact spot on the hole where the angler can get his bait to the bottom of the hole. He says, "Get the bait down in front of a fish and you will catch him."

On several occasions in every anglers life he will have the kind of day that on looking back it seems unreal. Dale Ivie recalls one: "On one occasion I was fishing a popular hole. First, I hooked into a small 8 pound jack salmon. Next, I hooked into a king which, after a 30 minute tug of war was landed and it weighed 41 pounds. After that it seemed as if I hooked a fish on every cast for in the next four hours I hooked, caught and released 17 more salmon and one or two of them were even bigger than my first keeper. The other anglers on the hole hardly did a thing, for again I was fortunate enough to be positioned so that my bait always swirled into the spot where the fish were grouped together."

When an angler fishes the streams for chinook, he fishes the same holes as for steelhead but he should fish them differently for best results. While the steelhead have a tendency to stay where the water is heavy, the salmon are generally down on the bottom in a pool where the water is at its absolute deepest point. Get the bait here and if there is a chinook in the pool your bait will be in front of it. Streams of course change character, holes change shapes and deepest points move about, but generally as the angler fishes from year to year he finds his spots and knows pretty much what he is looking for—this will improve his catches. A good idea is to study the stream when the water is low and then during high water you have an exact mental image of the spot.

Sometimes anglers will be standing along a stream and suddenly a big chinook will leap clear out of the water. It is an awesome sight, but if the angler were to take his bait and quickly cast it just in front of where the chinook jumped he may well get a strike. The fish will instinctively strike out at anything in the water, and if the hook is there it could very well nail him. Some anglers wonder why these fish jump and Mr. Ivie's thought on the matter is that the fish is lost and jumps to get a view of the surroundings. He says, "I have found the fish jumps to get a view of the surroundings. They generally jump when the water is murky. The salmon is trying to get back to the waters of its birth. It spent most of its life in the clear ocean and is now returning on the final trip of its life driven there by the desire to reproduce. When the fish suddenly finds itself in murky water with little visibility I feel this confuses the fish so that it rises up to the top of the water to jump clear and take a look. It may jump several times and will, at this time, instinctively strike at eggs or spinners presented to it. This isn't regular in fishing, but it does happen and it develops a quick opportunity to get a fish."

Bank fishing for salmon is done almost exactly the same way banking for steelhead is done. There seems to be more bank anglers for salmon. This is because the weather is often better and the salmon, being a bigger fish will battle the heavy tackle better.

One kind of fishing that is much more prevalent in salmon fishing than with steelheading is boat fishing. This is a great sport and on the Pacific coast it begins early in the springtime with the first runs of chinook. These anglers will continue picking up stray kings all through the summer.

This type of fishing is done in the Columbia from small boats generally 14 to 18 feet in length. The anglers head out into the river and anchor. Then they let out lines off the back of the boat letting them sink to the bottom and working them downstream in the current or bringing them upstream by reeling in. Often the boat anglers will shorten up on their rods, but many still use the standard 9 foot medium action salmon rod. The line used is usually 20 or 30 pound test monofilament and the terminal tackle works off a three way swivel. The weight line will be 12 to 30 inches long of 10 to 20 pound test and the size of weight tied on will vary from 4 to 16 ounces depending upon the river currents. The line leading from the swivel to the hook will be from 24 to 36 inches in length and it will usually include a spinner up in front of the bait or lure. Any standard spinner works and popular ones include a number 3 to 5 Colorado or Lucky-R, or Backmore. The spinners main function is to attract attention. He says, "My own preference in baits is to use one or two small 4 to 5 inch herrings which I put on the hook by running the hook through their mouths. In the water they will swim just as if they were alive. The bait will wobble and move about so that it looks very enticing to the salmon which will strike at it.

"I sometimes fish using a fly which I feel must be at least 2 inches in length. I generally use a big bucktail or a gaudy colored streamer that will imitate a baitfish. I have taken some nice fish on these as the salmon have a tendency to hit them hard.

"The one drawback of boat fishing is that the angler does not get the same fight out of the salmon as he would in a stream. This is simply a physical fact as the angler must tackle up heavier and often he will have heavy weights on the line all detracting from a fight, but kings are so strong they would give a good account of themselves against a winch."

During the summer boat fishing becomes popular along the coast and the prime fish is the cohoe. This smaller salmon is not a good upstream sportsfish but it certainly affords fine sport for the boat anglers at the Columbia mouth, throughout Puget Sound, Grays Harbor, Coos Bay, etc. It is strongly suggested that if the angler intends to charter out for summer fishing from spots such as Ilwaco on the Columbia that lodging and fishing reservations be made long in advance. This fishing has one advantage, for the beginner as it is probably the easiest way for anyone to get their first salmon as the skippers know their water and how to fish them.

Dale Ivie, like so many other fine anglers of the country, is worried about conservation. He looks at salmon and steelhead fishing, which he loves, and will fight violently to protect the fish. He points out that bad conservation habits and neglect have already cut big holes into the fish population of the West coast. In the early 1800's, commercial fishermen on the Columbia used 12 inch mesh nets about 1,500 feet long to take an estimated 2,000,000 pounds of salmon yearly. The fish then averaged 40 pounds each. Today the commercial anglers use 6½ inch mesh nets, and there are many more commercial fishermen whose total take still comes to 2,000,000 pounds of fish annually. The fishes average weight is only 18 pounds. He feels that stronger restrictions must be placed on commercial anglers to permit more fish to move upstream to the spawning areas. To show what commercial anglers can do to a run he points out that in several areas where the fish passed between two counting stations it was found that commercial fishermen had depleted 86% of the run. The highest catch ever recorded by sports anglers was 25% of a run. Also, Mr. Ivie feels the Indian treaty should be rewritten as Indians living in the Northwest are free to take fish anytime and by any method they chose. Many Indians have become commercial anglers selling their catches and depleting the supply terribly.

One of the most serious things is dam construction and he says it is deplorable to build a dam with no adequate fish ladders. The upper Snake River in Idaho, the North fork of the Lewis River, has been closed off by dams and of course Grand Coulie Dam has closed off vast areas of steelhead and salmon breeding waters. Mr. Ivie says, "No dam should be permitted to be constructed without adequate fish ladders." He points out that fish are a natural resource and they must be protected. He tells of seeing a run of salmon come up to a new dam and then just stay there without breeding waiting to die when they cannot pass to the waters of their birth. This may happen 3 to 4 years in a row until all generations of fish using these breeding waters are gone.

Lately the conservation departments have been capturing these trapped fish and artifically breeding the eggs, planting the fingerlings in other waters, but even this does not make up for the vast areas of breeding water lost.

Industrial waste, especially that of lumber and paper mills which dump refuse and chemicals into the water are another grave danger to the fishing. He says it is impossible to realize the full extent of the lethal effect on fish of industrial waste. One batch of waste can kill millions of fish in a vast area of a river. Mr. Ivie points directly at the Atlantic salmon which has disappeared from the East Coast of the United States as a result of a lack of conservation. He points out that each single item takes a great toll of fish and he warns Western anglers they must do everything possible to protect their fish or the fishing will disappear in our generation right in front of our eyes.

This fine sportsman writes letters to congressmen and state legislators, speaks, and is active in organizations such as the Association of Northwest Steelheads to fight the battle of conservation. He feels the least any angler should do is to support those organizations made up of dedicated men that are spending vast energies and trime to protect the fishing future of America.

5. TROUT FISHING WITH HARRY DARBEE

Mr. Harry Darbee lives on Route 17 near Livingston Manor right on one of New York State's most famous trout streams—the Willowemoc—a tributary of the Beaverkill. He is a conservationist and a fly fisherman by love who knows every hole, every fly hatch and every trick of taking trout on flies. Recently in *The New York Times* Mr. Darbee was referred to as "the dean of all trout anglers." He has been fly fishing for some 50 years yet by his own admission is still learning. The nicest thing about him is that if you met him on the stream or stopped in his home he would stop and talk fishing, giving advice and listening too, because trout fishing is his life. Harry Darbee is a professional fly tier whose flies are world famous and whose shop is a meeting ground for all kinds of anglers from the ultra purists to the out-and-out novices. His fishing ability, his knowledge of trout, his conservation efforts and his hospitality are famous.

He learned to love the outdoors as a boy and was always hunting, trapping, catching snakes, fishing or simply walking through the woods enjoying the sheer pleasure of outdoor life. Before he was twelve he had already become a fine angler and had graduated from bait fishing to fly fishing. Today he says, "Bait fishing is a

*** In 1964 Mr. Darbee won the Theodore Gordon Conservation Award.**

wonderful way for children to learn fishing but is a terrible way for a man to keep fishing." His specialty is fly fishing and he has taken brown trout, brook trout, rainbow trout, cutthroat trout and greyling in such varied places as Labrador, New Brunswick, Cape Breton, throughout New England, New York, Pennsylvania, Wisconsin, Minnesota, Wyoming, Montana, Tennessee and others.

This angler became a fly fisherman when at the age of ten he was given a cheap fly rod and a local resident showed him a unique way of taking trout. The method utilized a wet fly that was treated with mineral oil to help it float. The fly was cast across a stream and floated as a dry fly over a fish. Then as the float continued, the fly would be retrieved like a wet fly. Mr. Darbee recalls that the angler who showed him this method used only 3 fly patterns, yet consistently took big trout.

Harry Darbee is not a dry fly purist for he likes all phases of fly fishing—dry, wet, nymph, streamer and bucktail fishing. On one point Mr. Darbee is in direct contrast with the purists, for he feels that wet fly fishing demands more skill than even dry fly fishing. He says, "In dry fly fishing the angler knows exactly where his fly is and he can strike a fish properly for he sees the rise. However, with wet fly fishing, most of the time, the angler never sees the rise of the fish so he has no idea where his fly is and must learn to strike on feel. This is much more difficult.

"I don't care much for early season fishing," says Mr. Darbee, "because the fish are not ready. Early in the season the brookies and brownies have not had a chance to recover from their fall breeding which had taken so much out of them. During the winter the fish have been in a virtual state of hibernation and have hugged the bottom and lived off their own fat. They have not fed enough to recover their strength and weight so that on opening day in April they are skinny and weak. Often they are still in a state of semi-hibernation for it takes water over 50 degrees to get the trout out of their winter doldrums. I like to wait until the trout come off the bottom, spread themselves over a stream and get lively. Then they feed incessantly, rapidly gain strength and weight and are many times more sporty than a few short weeks before."

A typical yearly cycle of trout will find the fish sluggish in winter and early spring until the water warms up and the trout spread through the stream coming off the bottom. Fly hatches will be in their prime in the late spring (May on the Beaverkill), and fishing will be at its most productive point of the year. Then as summer approaches and the water level drops, the water temperature rises, and when it gets into the upper 60's, the trout slow up and look for pockets of cool water. They migrate considerable distances trying to find cooler water. Then they will be found in riffles, at the foot of pools or in shady spots with overhead protection from the sun. August is a danger month for trout because if the water should heat up too much many fish will die. The lethal temperature for brookies is 75 degrees, rainbows 80 degrees, and brownies 80 degrees, but even before these critical temperatures are reached many fish die. Mr. Darbee vigorously emphasizes that all conservation minded anglers must do everything in their power to protect our streams' natural flow and natural cover to help trout during this danger period. Summer fishing is difficult too for the water is usually extremely low, the fish are shy and when hooked they lack the vigor they had just a few weeks before.

One point this angler brings out is that some of the best trout fishing of the year takes place in the early fall. Many anglers don't fish in the fall but Harry Darbee feels they are missing some of the finest sport. He says, "In September the fish are in their prime. They have had a half year of steady feeding, they are in cool water and because they will soon be breeding they are in full strength and beauty. I've done some of my most enjoyable fishing at this time."

Although angler Darbee loves all phases of trout fishing, it is brown trout fishing that is closest to his heart. He says, "Brookies and rainbows are too gullible and make themselves too easy prey; but a brown trout is wary; he will stop feeding at the slightest suspicion and consequently becomes the sportiest to fish."

During any year, Harry Darbee will fish almost daily. He says, "I start many a trip dry fly fishing and going down to the stream to see what insects are hatching. I generally have a pretty good idea what will be out, but as soon as I see flies I begin the never ending game all trout anglers go through—matching the hatch. Next I look for rising fish and head right for them, for I try only to fish for large fish that are feeding. I don't want small fish. I prefer to give them a chance to grow up for they will be bigger the next time."

A typical day of fishing for Harry Darbee, about Memorial Day, would have him matching the many light colored insects on the stream. These can often be matched with a size No. 12 Light Cahill fly which is always a good starting selection then. There may be Caddis flies on the water, and in the early evening some Green Drakes and a few March Browns will be there. His favorite starting time is about 3 P.M. for this would be when the heaviest feeding begins.

Harry Darbee walks along the banks searching for such telltale signs as a ripple on the water or simply the shadow of a fish coming up. He often wears polarized sunglasses because this helps him to see the fish in the water as they come off the bottom. On the Beaverkill and Willowemoc he knows every hole and pool, but no matter where he fishes his method would be the same. He says, "Generally, I walk past 2 or 3 holes before I come to one where the right sized fish are feeding and when I find a spot I make a few casts over it. If the fish barrel up to hit the fly I know my neutral colored fly is the right one and I continue fishing. Flies like a No. 12 Light Cahill will look like many types of insects on the water and are therefore versatile.

"Should I take 5 or 10 casts over a rising fish without it going after the fly I know my choice of flies is wrong and I waste no more time and change patterns. My second choice at this time might be a March Brown (American) which is an excellent producer during May and June in this region. A few casts with this fly and again the process is repeated, if the fly takes fish I stay with it until the fish stop rising for it. If it does not take fish I make another change. Another possibility at this time is a Green Drake as there are often some of these insects about."

Mr. Darbee strongly advises a fly fisherman to keep moving along a stream going from pool to pool, always watching the water for rising fish. He feels it is important for an angler to concentrate his action only on feeding trout. There may be some afternoons when the angler may well feel he should have stayed in the cabin for an extra hour's nap for in spite of matching the hatch, seeing rising fish and making perfect presentations the fish still won't take the flies. If after a half a dozen patterns of various sizes have been tried and still no strikes, Mr. Darbee suggests forgetting all about the hatch and tying on a fly in direct contrast to what is hatching. A large spider fly, which could be so hairy that it makes you feel like spitting just to look at it, will sometimes get a reluctant fish to hit. Another excellent choice for wary fish is the Fan Wing Royal Coachman or any other brightly colored fly.

After the sun sets angler Darbee suggests there should be some Green Drakes on the water and a No. 12 fly of this pattern tied on a long shanked hook can be a deadly lure. If this fly should prove effective only on small fish and in the impending darkness, this angler suggests still another tactic. He feels the fisherman should try a large deer hair fly such as a white winged Rat Faced McDougal. This fly is floated directly over the fish and it should be twitched and moved gently as it moves over the trout. This big fly bouncing on the water can so rile up a fish that after four or five casts the trout may suddenly smash at the fly as if he wants to knock it clear to Australia. The White Winged Rat Faced McDougal is a thick deer hair fly and to the trout it may represent a fat female bug loaded with eggs while at other times it may simply irritate the fish into hitting. It often works.

As darkness closes in the dry fly angler does best by switching to large deer hair flies as these will be clearly visible as they float on the water. One of the bivisible flies will float high and have good visibility. Mr. Darbee suggests keeping a strip of amadou (amadou is a fungus and resembles leather), or simply some

Kleenex tissues handy and then when the fly gets wet lift it out of the water and squeeze it hard between this absorbent material to dry it out. This way a fisherman can go back to fishing without having to change flies which could be troublesome in the dusk. When darkness descends and the angler can no longer see the fly on the water it is time to quit dry fly fishing. Should he continue to hear the fish jumping and he wants to go on fishing it is best to switch to wet flies for these can be fished all night long.

During the warm weather of July the insect hatches will be fewer in number than earlier in the season. The size of the insects will be smaller with a few notable exceptions which will be very large insects. If there should be hatches of stone flies, or May flies on the water, to match them, the angler should consider using flies No. 12 to 14. As the torrid weather arrives, there will be even fewer aquatics on the water and those that are there will be smaller. Generally small brightly colored flies sizes No. 12 to 16 will be the best fish producers during the hot months. These flies should be bright in color using such patterns as the Gold Ribbed Hare's Ear, the Lead Wing Coachman and of course, the Royal Coachman. Often spiders are on the water then, and a spider taken from the fly packet may work wonders. Flies that imitate inchworms, or that look like a dragon fly or another large winged insect, can often raise trout at this time. During the hot weather it is less important to match the hatch as the fish will not be consistently feeding on any one type of fly.

Mr. Darbee explains that the tactics of a summer angler call for him working either up or downstream while he keeps a sharp lookout for rising fish. The water will be low and the large fish will be found mostly in the deep pools and pockets. They are likely to be in any spot where there is cover from the sun. This sometimes calls for strange casts when a fly has to be presented under some overhanging branches.

According to Mr. Darbee there isn't a place on a stream where the angler cannot cast a fly. One of the tricks he sometimes uses when all other methods of presentation fail is to simply get directly upstream from the fish and let his fly float down in the water right over the rising fish. Mr. Darbee explains this method is excellent when going for some exceptionally shy fish that may be resting in clear, still or very shallow water. He says, "One of the anglers tried for three days for a big rainbow in a mirror like pool. He said that no one could rise that fish. I bet him $10 I could. I got upstream at least 100 yards from the fish and let my fly float down to Mr. Rainbow. All my fly line was out plus part of the 150 yards of backing I kept on my reel before the fly reached the trout. I saw the fly was passing right over the rainbow and sure enough he boiled and hit the fly. It is extremely difficult to set a hook at this distance and generally the fish has to hook itself. I missed the fish, but I made my point for I raised this otherwise inaccessible fish by this unorthodox method."

During the hot weather the heavy fast riffles always offer a fly fisherman good water for trout fishing and often it is the best spot an angler can fish. Mr. Darbee says, "If a beginner or an occasional weekend fisherman were to exclusively fish the riffles they would catch fish, but good anglers should not do this for they lose too many opportunities for big fish in other kinds of water. Generally during the summers, the first third of the pools are where the fish are, and an angler only fishes the lower third if he happens to see fish rising there. Most of the time this is dead water.

Fisherman Darbee warns that very often anglers will approach some fish and scare them. He says, "An angler should approach a fish only as close as he has to so that he is able to get a decent cast to the fish. This may be 30, 40, or 60 feet. The browns are the most shy and will be most easily spooked, therefore they need special caution on the approach. The best way is, of course, from the rear for the fish will be facing upstream and in this way the angler will be outside his cone of vision. Generally the most practical way is to the rear and to the side. The fly is thrown up in front of the fish so that it floats back over him. It is better to throw the fly too far in front of a fish than too close to him where the possibility of getting it behind his striking area exists. I remember once sitting on the banks and watching a particular angler go for a nice sized brown trout that was rising. This fish was infuriating this angler, for he wouldn't touch a single fly presented. What was happening was very visible from where I sat on the bank. The angler was casting to the point where he saw the trout rise. In this case it was too close to the fish because on each rise this brownie would move upstream about a yard, choose a bug and then follow it down a yard or so before he took it. After that angler gave up in disgust I went over and took that fish on the very first cast. I remember this because it proved how important it is to cast up ahead of a fish. This angler had thought his troubles were fly selections which just wasn't so, for his mistake was not putting the fly far enough ahead of the fish."

The strong, heavy, vigorous trout of September really tempt anglers like Harry Darbee to get out after them. The insect life is usually small and short lived in the fall and fly sizes run from No. 14 to 16. Good beginning fly selections are neutral colored flies of the same favorite patterns of spring and summer. If no hits occur, again a dramatic color change, or an irritating fly may really stir up these high strung trout.

This expert angler says that all types of trout can be taken by following the basic principles just outlined. However if the quarry is brookies, he adds one suggestion: always have a supply of black flies on hand. He says, "Brookies live best in the upper reaches of a river or in cold lakes. Generally the lower sections of streams and rivers are denied the brookie because of his cold water demands. There are usually black gnats on brookie waters, therefore the angler should supply his fly box with a generous amount of Black Gnats, Black Midges, and other assorted black fly patterns. The Black Gnat, size No. 14 to 20, is the most important of these and it is often murder on these energetic strikers.

"There are certain things a good dry fly angler can do when he runs into a situation where there are no fish rising," says Mr. Darbee. "I find a good spot on the stream where I know there are fish and then artificially begin orienting the fish to rising for insects. I pick a fly out of my tackle box and cast it over the fish not even expecting them to rise. I cast to the same spot time and time again always getting the same float over the fish. I may cast 20, 50, or 150 times if necessary, but somewhere along the line a fish will begin to rise for the fly. What happens is that this fly passes over the fish so often they have become accustomed to seeing it and eventually it registers as a fly hatch to them. Then one will rise for the fly.

"Another trick that can be tried on uncooperative fish is to use a Neversink Skater. This fly may well be the strangest of any ever tried as it is about as big as a silver dollar and it is made with very stiff hackles that are spread out and tied onto a very tiny No. 16 hook. This fly is cast out over some trout and twitched on the water with the angler continually keeping it bouncing and moving. If the fish are close to shore and the angler can remain concealed, he can merely bounce it from the end of his rod. Often after this fly has made several runs over some trout the fish will get all riled up and will come up and really smash the daylights out of this irritating thing. Fish are seldom hooked on the fly for the hackles get in the way of the small hook and therefore it is used more to rile fish up and get them to come up. What the angler does after he gets the trout to rise with this fly is to quickly change to a normal dry fly and work on the fish to hit that. I have got them so excited by this fly that they would hit anything after that."

This expert angler says, "When an angler scares fish and they stop feeding this doesn't mean he can no longer catch those fish. Fish get scared a thousand times a day from a slight ripple on the water or a shadow or just from some visible movement that is enough to put a trout off feed. As soon as I see I have put a trout off feed I stop moving and just stand. Almost all anglers are aware that fish stop feeding very easily, but many do not realize that they will begin to feed again almost as easily if not further disturbed. Some fish will resume feeding within a minute, but other times I may have to wait 5 minutes for them to start rising again, and on occasions I've waited as much as 15 minutes for one to feed again. The stream is a beautiful place to be and it is always worth waiting for a big one."

Harry Darbee considers the wet fly to be the most perfect

man-made lure. He, like millions of fly tiers before him, is proud of the fact that with a hook, feathers, hair and some thread, he can make the most productive lures ever devised by man. The wet fly is so versatile that it can be made to imitate dead insects in the water, live insects that just fell in the water, insects that are immature and have not left the water. The wet fly in the form of streamers and bucktails imitate minnows perfectly.

The wet flies that imitate insects will be tied with soft absorbent materials so that they quickly sink under the surface of the water when fished. They must be fished at the level the fish are feeding—anywhere from an inch under the surface right to rolling them along the bottom. Some anglers add a piece of shot to their leader when they want their fly deep, but Mr. Darbee doesn't like this, for he feels it takes much of the natural float of a fly away from it. When he wants his fly deep he prefers to give it plenty of time to sink, using sinking line to take it down. At times he ties some lead weight right into the flies themselves, for the weighted fly will act far more natural than one where the shot is a foot or so up on the leader.

During the early spring, when the water is cold and high and the fish are concentrated in pools, the weighted fly is the best choice. The angler fishes his flies at the heads of the pools and he works his flies so that they sink down deep enough to reach the fish. One of the common mistakes is not getting the lure deep enough.

The best method for fishing a wet fly is to throw it up and across stream to give it time to sink to the desired depth as it sweeps to the fish. Sometimes very large bends will begin to develop in the line and to get them out the angler must mend his line. He does this by flipping the rod tip over and upstream and taking in the slack. The upstream flip of the rod tip is repeated as the fly works downstream. This flip has another effect for it gives motion to the fly in the water and this often helps attract a fish. The motion is particularly effective whenever there are flies that were just swept into the water and they are still alive trying to get airborn again.

During the spring if the caddis flies are hatching they will bounce all over the water and the angler should fish his fly with plenty of motion. The fish will be looking for it because they are chasing lively insects. The procedure is to keep twitching the rod tip to give the fly motion in the water. Spent May flies will at times be at all levels of water and here the angler fishes his fly by simply letting it drift in the current to the fish.

Among some fine producers before June 15th are the Lead Wing Coachman, the Gold Ribbed Hares Ear, and of course, a Blue Dun. These flies in sizes No. 10 to 14 will take any kind of trout swimming during this early season and they will continue to be producers all year long on a slightly reduced degree. Mr. Darbee tells wet fly anglers that they should use longer leaders for this fishing and he usually prefers a tapered leader of 12 feet utilizing a 5X Tippet.

Special water conditions call for a change of tactics. If the water gets turbid, the angler should switch to larger flies using No. 4 or 6 size and he should use the brightest colored patterns in his fly box generally favoring the yellows, reds and oranges. Trout are attracted by color, for they see color well and in water where visibility may be somewhat limited it often makes the difference. If the angler is fishing a very large stream with turbulent water, he should again fish the large flies. However, bright colors are not so important here for the fish will hit the more neutral colored flies readily. The angler fishing after dark should again use large sized flies, sizes No. 2 to 8, of highly visible patterns.

This expert angler has one word of advice for all fly fishermen and that is, proper presentation of a fly is far more important than fly selection. He says, "There are now so many fly patterns, some of which vary so slightly that I'm sure a fish can not tell them apart. However, gross errors in patterns or size will have a fish pass up a fly, yet, in my experience I have found that improper presentation was the biggest cause of no hits. I feel if the angler presents the fly directly to the fish and the fish is feeding then it will take any reasonable facsimile of the current food supply." Mr. Darbee emphasizes, "The most important thing is that the angler must show the fly to a fish!"

Summer wet fly fishing calls for the same general pattern of flies as the dry fly angler uses except in this instance they will be the wet fly version of these patterns. Other fine producers are such bright starlets as the Wickmans Fancy or a Queen of the Water, which is a real attention getter in low clear water. Size of flies in the summer generally run from No. 12's to 16's with the angler going to the smaller ones as the water level drops off to its lowest point. Harry Darbee suggests the angler get an exceptionally small fly, possibly a 16 or even smaller, and then in low water conditions fish this right along the bottom at the head of pools. The fish will be low in these cool sections of the stream and when one of these flies drifts in front of them they will grab. The tiny fly can be exceptionally productive fished this way.

Occasionally an angler can see fish splashing about in an apparent frenzy of hitting surface insects. This generally calls for a plunge into the dry fly patterns but when these are fished they may produce absolutely nothing. If the angler inspects the situation very carefully he may find that the fish are merely breaking the surface with their tails and are diving down to grab at the immature insects coming off the bottom. A wet fly fished along the bottom or a nymph fished in the same manner will produce a good string of trout in this situation. The important thing is for the angler to be able to recognize what is happening and fish accordingly.

The wet fly patterns suitable for fall fishing are the same ones that are used in dry fly fishing. The flies being as small as the insects will generally be small. In some cases there will be no hatch to match, therefore, a colorful fly drifted in the water will attract the fish and have them smash at it. Trout will be found at all levels varying from situation to situation, so that the angler should remain on the alert trying to spot the fish and then fish to them.

Those anglers fishing bucktails and streamers will be fishing flies that are imitating minnows. Their best basic maneuver is to cast upstream and across stream and then allow a long slow downstream drift trying to work the fly deep into the pools. While the fly is drifting downstream the angler should mend his line as this will get slack out of the line and it will give the fly that sudden jerky action so true of minnows in the water. An angler fishing bucktails and streamers should have at least 4 or 5 patterns to work with. Mr. Darbee suggests a basic collection including a Black Ghost, a Black and White, a Yellow Gold, a White, a Brown and White, and a red one with a silver body. A popular bucktail pattern he suggests is a Delaware Bucktail and a Summer Gold. He gives anglers one word of caution and that is when a fly raises a fish and gets him chasing the fly, but somehow he never hits it that fly is not fooling the fish. The angler should change patterns for this may help.

Some streamers imitate colorful dragon flies or very large stone flies, and whenever these insects are about these flies are good.

A somewhat new technique which has worked well for Harry Darbee is tying both a streamer and a dry fly on the same leader. Here he generally uses 12 feet of leader and 4 feet from the bottom he ties a bright fly such as a Royal Coachman, while at the end of the leader he puts on a Black and White streamer or a Yellow and Gold one. This package is thrown out and floated downstream and kept moving on the water. The dry fly is there to attract the attention of the fish. When they come up at it, they suddenly see a bigger dinner that is even easier to take and they strike! Mr. Darbee tells of the luck he has had with this combination and on several occasions he has even had doubles, "Once I had a brown hit the streamer and as soon as he pulled the dry fly under a rainbow came up and hooked himself on the Coachman—what a headache that was." On another occasion he had doubles of rainbows and once a brown and a bass took it simultaneously. Other times the fish will take the dry fly, which in this case is really put there as a teaser to attract attention. He has pointed out that no matter what fly the fish takes, this particular combination has filled his creel often and it is worth a try for anyone.

"Whether the angler is fishing dry, wet, or streamer flies he must give the fish time to take the fly," says this expert. "I feel an angler will lose many fish by striking too swiftly and if it comes to a choice of striking too fast or too slow, too slow is by far the lesser error to make. A strike made too swiftly snatches the fly from the fish before he gets it in his mouth while the strike made too slowly often doesn't matter for many fish hook themselves anyway. The right procedure is to lift the rod tip as it bends from the strike. This is a short lift merely tightening the line. If it hooks the fish correctly it will get him right in the corner of the mouth. This will hold a fish through any kind of a fight but the real beauty of it is that after the fight the angler can slide the small hook out of the fishes mouth just as easily as if he were taking it out of butter. This gentle handling of the fish permits the all important releases which give the small fish a chance to grow up and the big ones that you don't keep will get a chance to breed again." Mr. Darbee feels the worst part of bait fishing for trout isn't that flies are so much sportier, it is simply that bigger hooks are generally used and that trout swallow baits deeply so that it injures a fish and they die even if released.

Once the fly is struck and the angler hears a zinging in his line he needs no one to tell him that he is into a beauty. But Mr. Darbee warns that all too many anglers actually lose the very big fish that they wait a lifetime to hook, and they lose them from unpreparedness and over anxiety. "When a fish first hits," Harry Darbee says, "he is either on or he isn't. If the hook is properly set it won't make a difference at this time if the angler gives the fish all the slack line he wants, for that hook will have just set in the fish and until actual tight contact is made the fish won't be able to spit it. Usually a fish will hit and if he doesn't immediately run he heads for the bottom to sulk. Slack line now helps the angler for it gives him a few precious seconds to get himself in order, retreat to a place of good footing, get twists out of the line or anyone of a dozen things that must be done. Once the line is tightened the fight will begin in earnest and now it becomes important to keep a tight line on a fish and not give him slack. If the fish is big, he will run and he could run long and hard so that the angler must be prepared to scamper along and he must have ample line to let the fish run. The perfect position is to get on the downstream side of the fish and stay there pulling the fish gently downstream and to the side to tire him out. If the angler can stay slightly downstream, any fish, no matter what his size, becomes the anglers prize. When a trout is spent he should be carefully lead into the net. He is then your trophy."

Trout fisherman Harry Darbee has very special likes and dislikes in his tackle selections. One item where he differs radically with most authorities is on the reel. Mr. Darbee says, "An angler should get an expensive light reel for this is all important in taking trout." He knows this will lift some eyebrows higher than a receding hair line but he explains, "many anglers merely strip line in when they have a trout on and for them the reel is nothing more than a convenient place to store line. These anglers just never took a large trout for a big rainbow would run that standard 30 yards of fly line off this reel so fast that the angler would hardly have time to lament his lost fish. Big fish have to be fought off the reel just as they are in other fishing, in fact, I take all my fish in off the reel now. I used to strip them in until I hooked into one giant rainbow, and when I lost him that quickly cured me of this habit.

"To cope with a large trout the angler should have a reel large enough to hold his 30 to 35 yards of fly line plus 50 to 150 yards of backing which I think should be 8 to 10 pound test line. If the reel is small I reduce the test to 6 pounds or less, but I want at least 100 yards of extra line there when I need it. I may not need the backing for a whole season but when a big one wants to get out of a pool there is nothing anyone can do but let him go and that extra yardage of backing will be what allows me time to scamper after him—it makes the difference."

Mr. Darbee says, "For line I like either 30 or 35 yards of Doubled Tapered silk line depending on whether I use the English Tapered or American Lines. As for this line, I prefer the best oil finished lines so that more often than not I use the English ones as they taper down to a very fine diameter. Occasionally when I'm dry fly fishing I use the bubble lines to utilize their high float. For most of my fishing I use silk lines as it is the best all around. My backing is braided nylon casting line.

"Leader is of course extremely important for it must be as nearly invisible as possible while being strong enough to hold the fish. The leader is the weakest link between the angler and his fish and broken lines generally occur at the leader. To get maximum deception from my leader I use at least 9 feet of leader and go to 12 feet for wet fly fishing and for fly fishing with low water conditions. The tapered gut leaders are best, but I use the synthetics too. For a tippet I like 14 to 16 inches of 4X gut which has the greatest strength under shock as it will give on a sudden hit. The gut will resist breaking on the strike better than any other material but of course good gut is scarce and hard to get so as an alternate I like 5X playtl. This makes a strong fine diameter tippet that is very limp and allows excellent fly presentation. I do much of my fishing with Playtl tippets now.

"As for a rod there is nothing like a well made bamboo rod for fly fishing," says Harry Darbee. "These rods are exceptionally expensive going to about $150 each as the craftsmen who make them are getting very scarce. There are few new rodmakers entering the field.

"I use a stiff, so-called tip action rod, which is not the fast tip action of glass rods, but rather a bamboo rod in which most of the action is in the upper two-thirds of its length—the butts are quite stiff. My preference is for this rod because the action seems to suit my own muscular reaction. I would tire quickly using any other action and most folks would tire easily using the rods I prefer. The rods I use are made by H. S. (Pinky) Gillum of Ridgefield, Connecticut. I believe he ranks with Payne, Garrison, Edwards and others of America's famous rod makers."

Harry Darbee suggests, "For anyone wanting one superb fly rod I would suggest an 8½ foot bamboo rod made by one of the master craftsmen. Special rods such as 7 footers for small brookie streams or 10 to 12 footers for salmon fishing are another story for each of these are designed for a very definite and special purpose. The angler that gets an 8½ footer of bamboo will have a versatile trout rod he will be proud of."

Mr. Darbee's trout fishing and his fly tying are famous, but his work in trout conservation has now reached legendary proportions. He has worked long hard hours to preserve fishing waters throughout the Catskill region. Some of his hardest fights have been waged against the building of dams. Dams are built and the flow of water from them can be regulated at will and in some anywhere from 4 million to 100 gallons of water can be released in a day. Sudden changes of temperature are lethal to fish and in the summers when the gates are suddenly opened to release terminal cold water from the bottom of the lake to roar into the warmer shallow water below the dam it kills fish all along the way.

Mr. Darbee tells of the effect of temperature changes on fish: "Fishing one summer, I spotted a rainbow trout that had taken refuge in a cold spot in the bottom of the stream, the low temperature being caused by spring seepage in the river bottom. The flows around this spring, both above and on all sides, were above 80 degrees. The fish rose to the fly, leaving the cold water, and attempted to return to his lie in this spring flow. This, of course, I prevented, and in the ensuing battle which lasted a very few minutes, the fish actually died before I could land it. I have had similar occurrences on other occasions."

He says, "As a result of dam building the sports fishery below the Neversink Dam and below the East Branch of the Delaware no longer exists as it was before the dams were built. Today the State of New York stock trout below each dam. They are available to anglers as long as conditions allow for their survival. This, of course, is unpredictable since minimum flows during warm summer months produce temperatures beyond the lethal level for trout. Further, the smallmouth bass which did inhabit both streams have not survived the extremely low temperatures during high releases from these dams. They no longer reproduce in the East Branch of the Neversink and bass fishery has disappeared.

Two great Catskill fishing streams have been lost as a result of damming them. A third, the West Branch of the Delaware, is in the process of going the same way. The loss of fishing could probably be alleviated when future dams are planned providing a serious attempt is made to consider the ecology of the stream and the future of the fisheries below the dams. If a warm flow were steadily maintained during summer months, I believe bass could survive. If a cold flow on the other hand was steadily maintained, there could be no doubt about the benefit to trout, but even this could never restore the lost fisheries as they once existed. One or the other of these species (bass or trout) would have to go."

Another battle Mr. Darbee waged was against DDT spraying. "We sportsmen opposed the spraying on the grounds that it was harmful to the organisms in the stream upon which fish must depend for food. Owing to a vigorous campaign by the Beamoc Club, of which I am Conservation Chairman, neither the Beaverkill nor the Willowemoc Valleys were sprayed. In other areas I was present during part of the spraying and later picked up a great many dead fish which were put in formaldehyde and others were frozen. I later was a witness in the DDT hearing held before the United States District Court in the much publicized DDT hearing in Brooklyn. This case was lost by the landowners and others who sued because of contamination of pastures, vegetable gardens, fish ponds, death of birds and other wild life but the decision resulted in Justice Douglas filing a vigorous dissent when the Supreme Court reviewed the decision of the District Court. There is little likelihood of a similar massive spraying being undertaken in the same high-handed manner in the future."

One fight Mr. Darbee is proud of, "There is one major battle we have won. This was a fight to stop dumping in the Beaverkill where garbage, unwanted earth, cinders, ashes and the like were being thrown directly into the stream and on its banks at dozens of points. The dumpers were persistent and it took national publicity to get this nuisance abated. The result was a bill which became law prohibiting the dumping of any solids other than snow

HARRY DARBEE'S FAVORITE DOZEN

NAME	QUILL GORDON	LIGHT CAHILL	MARCH BROWN	HENDRICKSON	WHITE WINGED RAT FACED McDOUGAL	BLUE DUN
WING	Wood Duck	Wood Duck	Heavily Barr Dark Mandarin or Wood Duck	Wood Duck	White Hair (Calftail)	Slate Duck Quill
TAIL	Dun Hackle Fibers	Pale Ginger Hackle Fibers	Dark Hackle Ginger Fibers	Light Blue Dun Hackle Fibers	Ginger Hackle Fibers	Soft Blue Dun Fibers
BODY	Striped Peacock Quill and Ribbed Fine Silver Wire	Cream Colored Fox Fur	Light Tan Fox Fur	Light Tan Fox Fur	Clipped Grayish Tan Deer Hair	Medium Blue Muskrat Fur
HACKLES	Blue Dun	Pale Ginger	1 Dark Plymouth Rock (Grizzly) 1 Dark Ginger	Light Blue Dun	Ginger	Soft Blue Dun
SIZE	20 to 8	20 to 8	20 to 8	Smallest Sizes to Imitate the Naturals, sizes 18 to 12 all useful	14-8	20 to 6
TYPE	Dry or Wet	Dry or Wet	Dry or Wet	Dry or Wet	Dry	Wet
BEST USE	Throughout Season	Spring but Good all Season Matches Light Hatches	Late Spring	Early Season but Usable Anytime	June to End of Season	Throughout Season

TROUT FLIES AND DRESSING

GOLD RIBBED HARE'S EAR	*LEAD WING COACHMAN*	*FAN WING COACHMAN*	*DUN VARIANT*	*BLACK GHOST*	*DELAWARE*
Light Slate Duck Quill	Dark Slate Duck Quill	2 Feathers White from Breast of Mandarin or Woodduck	None	4 White Matched Hackles Jungle Cock Cheeks With Head of Black Laquer	Lemon Yellow Bucktail 1/3rd Longer than Hook Tied Sparsely on underside of hook and 6 or 8 strands of Peacock Herl on topside same Length at Bucktail over which Brown Bucktail Head, Black Laquer
Brown Hackle Fibers	None	Golden Phesant Tippet Fibers	Dun Hackle Fibers	Lemon Yellow Hackle Fibers	None
Hares Ear Fur Ribbed With Flat Gold Tinsel	Peacock Herl	Equal 1/3: 1, Peacock Herl 2, Red Silk Floss 3, Peacock Herl	Brown Hackle Quill	Black Silk Floss Ribbed With Flat Silver Tinsel	Embossed Gold Tinsel
Hares Fur Picked Out at Throat With Dubbing Needle	Soft Light Brown	Medium Brown	Dun	Lemon Yellow	None
16 to 6	16 to 6	14 to 8	16 to 10	Long Shanked 12 to 4	Long Shanked 14 to 10
Wet	Wet	Dry	Dry	Streamer Fly	Bucktail
All Season	All Season	All Season	All Season	All Season	All Season

or ice in the trout streams of New York State. This law was later broadened to include the banks of the streams also if the dumped material could reach the water at any stage of flow. Here the Beamoc Club was joined by many organizations and individuals. Articles appeared in the newspapers all over the country, outdoor magazines, and particularly in *Sports Illustrated.* The result was one of the greatest conservation achievements in New York State in many years and, believe me, we were only entitled to a small portion of the credit."

In spite of all our errors and in spite of increasing population Mr. Darbee says, "Sports fishing for trout could be better today than it was 30 years ago." His explanation for this is that there are many marginal farms in the mountain country that have been abandoned and new forest land and cover is growing up here. As a result we are getting cooler streams that are better able to propagate trout. He also feels future improvement will hinge on sportsmen emphasizing fishing for trout as a sport rather than for the table. Then Mr. Darbee says "If we have good conservation practices and we sportsmen fight to save our streams there should be trout fishing in this country for years to come." If everyone fights as hard as this superb angler there will be an increase in trout fishing everywhere.

SALTWATER FISHING

6. STRIPED BASS FISHING WITH DAVID AND ROSA WEBB

The world's oldest fishing record, the 73 pound striped bass taken by Charles Church in 1913, will soon be topped. This is the opinion of virtually all the leading striper anglers of New England and they base this on the fact that a revolutionary method of fishing is being used by the Cape Cod striper anglers that is really getting the lunkers to hit the line.

New England anglers feel that the East coast of Massachusetts is the best striper fishing water in the world and they proudly point out that 4 out of 5 of the largest fish ever taken came from these waters. Their feeling that the world's record fish will soon come from here is backed up by the records too, for during a recent 5 year period 10 of the 20 largest stripers on record, all over 63 pounds, were taken here in Eastern Massachusetts. The best fishing here is concentrated along the beach front running from Nauset Beach, near Orleans to Race Point, just east of Provincetown, a distance of less than 50 miles.

David and Rosa Webb, of Shrewsbury, Massachusetts, have watched all the modern developments of striper fishing from its crude beginnings to the sophisticated specialty fishing of today.

Dave Webb remembers going to the water with his grandfather and there with a simple drop line swinging a weight around his head and throwing a hook soaked with worms out to the water. When a fish was hooked, it was handlined in. Later, immediately after World War II, Dave introduced his wife Rosa to the sport and luckily she took to it like a beachcomber. The very first time she went fishing Rosa took a small 10 inch bass, but it wasn't easy for her in spite of fishing every weekend and three weeks of solid vacation fishing she didn't catch another striper for another four years. Most girls would have been thoroughly disgusted, but she just kept fishing. Her eyes will light up and she says, "One morning while everyone was still asleep I decided to fish a little so I cast out and something hit my line. I was excited and nervous and the fish fought like a demon but I landed him and had my first 10 pound striper." This broke the ice, and after that Rosa Webb was on her way to becoming one of the leading lady anglers of the country and holder of the women's all tackle record for stripers.

The Webb's fishing spot in those days was famous Nauset Beach. They would drive to Orleans and then drive as close to the beach as they could get their car and from there they walked to the fishing areas of the beach. Considering this was walking through the kind of sand that could tire out a camel and considering it meant carrying a whole alignment of fishing tackle including rods, reels, lures, lines, extra reels, baits as well as waders, weather proof parkas, hoods and other clothing, it was anything but a luxury trip. Then, it meant fishing and working anywhere from 1 to 2 miles of beach while continually casting and working the lures with the heavy stiff tackle of those days. After fishing it meant a dog tired trudge back to the car with possibly 20 to 50 pounds of fish to take back. To make things more difficult much of the walking was done at night for this is always the best time for surf fishing as the fish come in closer after dark. Still this did not daunt the army of surf casters for during the 26 weeks of the striper season the same anglers came back to their regular stands week after week.

Beach buggies started to make things easier for surf anglers beginning about 1949. The Webb's got their first buggy in 1950 and with it they were able to carry all their equipment right to the spot they intended to fish. Their first buggy was an old Chevy which they stripped to make it as light as possible and they added oversized wheels to pull the car out of the sand. The early theories of buggies was that lightness allowed them to skip over the sand. Soon this theory was turned right around, and now buggies are heavy but with oversized tires and four wheel drive they can be pulled out of any sand on the beach. The Webb's latest beach buggy is a summer home camper. They have an 8 by 9 foot cabin, complete with a bed, stove and refrigerator, mounted on a FC 170 Jeep Truck. Their rods are in rod holders fastened to the front end of the Jeep and they look like a string of antennas. In addition they now carry a 12 foot aluminum boat and outboard with them on every beach trip.

About 1955 the Webb's changed from Nauset to the less crowded Provincetown beaches as their base of operation. Now they take their camper down to Race Point in the spring and leave it there to live in throughout the striper season. David Webb built their particular cabin himself, but these have really caught on and manufacturers are making many models the same type now. When they fish their buggy goes down to the beach and they bring it as close to the water as possible. The four wheel drive of the jeep pulls them out of any sand and several times they have had to back out of places with the water up to the hubcaps. Life in their camper is comfortable for they have a warm sleeping room even on the coldest nastiest Cape Cod nights. Then after a night of fishing their cabin on wheels is as luxurious as the best hotel in the world.

The stripers migrate along the Atlantic coast moving North to the New England waters and the first striper is annually taken in this Eastern portion of Cape Cod about the middle of May. This officially begins the striper fishing season here. Then fishing picks up a little and in some years there is an excellent run in June while other years the pickings are lean. July usually spells fairly good fishing which extends into August. Sometime after the middle of August and going into September is the best time for fishing for this is when the biggest and most fish are taken. It is just before the major migration South that this fishing occurs. Then there will be some fishing in October and sometimes it extends into November, but it will be at a much slower pace than the big late summer and early fall run. Sometimes during a very warm fall when the water remains warm there will be fishing right into late November and some diehards will even take stripers off Southern Massachusetts and Rhode Island as late as the middle of December.

The regular fishermen consider striper fishing of Cape Cod a 26 weeks season hitting its peak sometime in late August or September. It is always important for the regular anglers to know when the fishing will be at its absolute peak and intricate charts of water temperatures, moon cycles and past histories of catches have been kept by many of the surfmen. They try desperately to time their vacation weeks so that it coincides perfectly with the times of the biggest catches.

David Webb traditionally takes his vacation in late August and has it fall during a period of a full moon for he says, "Striper fishing from shore is always best during a full moon for it brings the high tides and the fish come closest to shore then."

Striper fishing is always changing. It has changed from very early times when it was a rich man's sport where areas were chummed and fishing stands that were somewhat similar to duck shooting stands were constructed on rocks. The anglers placed themselves on the stands, sometimes tying themselves in them so that they wouldn't be swept out to sea, and fished. This way they were able to work an incoming tide with their crude equipment. Some anglers used handlines, but finally rods and reels came into prevalence. The early rods were heavy and might measure 12 to 15 feet and the reels were stiff and hard while the line was thick linen. This was heavy bulky tackle difficult to manipulate and almost impossible for anyone but the strongest anglers to fish with. Rosa Webb recalls her early fishing troubles stemmed a great deal from the equipment for the rods were heavy and stiff and the reels no help either. She recalls most women just couldn't cast this tackle far enough to be effective fishermen.

Today, both David and Rosa, use the same equipment—a #542 Harnell Rod which measures 10 feet and will do all the heavy duty fishing required of it while it still remains a sporty rod. Both use a Penn Squidder #140 reel which they load with 150 yards of 36 or 45 pound nylon line. They double the last 15 feet of line as this section nearest the hook takes the worst abuse. This is the standard tackle for their regular fishing and they use it except for special times. One of these special times is when a large number of school sized fish come near shore when they whip out spinning rods with 306 and 300 Garcia reels. This tackle is perfect for 2 to 10 pound fish.

The bait end of the tackle is where the really big and constant changes have been made. "Each year is a new adventure for baits and lures that really take the fish will continually change," says Rosa Webb. "We start each year with the favorite bait or lure of the year before and sometimes we find the fish are not interested in that anymore. Then someone will start catching fish—usually bigger fish and more fish than the other regulars of the beach. We ask him how he got them and when his answers are evasive we know he is on to something new. He is a marked man for everyone on the beach will be watching him. It won't take long and his new lure or bait or method is observed and then word will spread around like wildfire and within a few days everyone will be trying it. If it takes fish it will become the sensation of the season and in some years it may even completely change the style of fishing." It was just such a move that brought a recent development to Cape Cod striper fishing and this made possible the biggest and largest catches ever.

Right after World War II when striper surf fishing got back into high gear the anglers started by fishing with plugs. These out of necessity had to be big for they were fished with the stiff tackle of the day. Some of the plugs used then were the Captain Bill plugs and some anglers fashioned their own plugs out of broomsticks. A section of broomstick 6 to 9 inches long would be cut and the front of the plug angled while the back would be rounded off. Two or three sets of treble hooks would be added and a coat of paint slapped on and the angler had himself a going plug that worked similar to a Reverse Atom plug, another popular plug of those days. As the tackle lightened the plugs got smaller. One year the plugs were getting anglers nowhere and just to pass time one angler rigged a small eel on a hook and threw it out. The result was astonishing for he got hit after hit. After that everyone finished the season with that bait. Another year the sensation was a Stinkey Atom which was a lure that is loaded with scent and as it is dragged through the water it makes its own chum line. This lure too lost its appeal a year or so later. Another year it was a marine worm that did the trick and so on change after change.

During the year 1953 the first surf anglers appeared out at the beach with some pontoon boats. They reasoned that the really big fish were out just beyond the first breaker where most of the time the anglers just couldn't reach from shore. They started having success and one of the first lures that paid off in this kind of fishing was a Creek Chub. Here the boys learned to weight the nose of the lure down so that it would move through the water 5 to 6 feet under the surface. The bass would come up and smash at the lure. Fishing was good in the pontoon boats, but some funny things happened with them and one day some boys lost all their tackle and had themselves a fine swim when one of them gaffed the boat instead of the fish he was bringing in.

Soon after that wooden and aluminum boats began to show up with outboard motors attached. Aluminum was found light and easy to handle on the beaches so they quickly became the most popular type boat. There was great resistance among traditional surf anglers to join the boat brigade but when they started witnessing some of the catches that were being brought back even the most reluctant gave serious thoughts to investing in a boat. One of the first methods used by the boat anglers to get stripers was by dragging a sea worm along the bottom. The bass lying there would lunge out and grab the worm. This fishing was done with wire line and the worm was hooked onto a No. 1 or No. 2 hook so that it trailed behind. This method is still used today and some of the anglers now drag one or two plastic worms along as they look and feel so much like the real thing it is impossible for man or fish to tell the difference. Still most anglers add a real worm to the package or will add at least a piece of worm for they feel the fishes sense of taste and their sensitive sense of smell will be attracted by the real worm.

David and Rosa Webb bought themselves a 12 foot aluminum boat and with some reluctance they left the shore and started to work outside of the breakers. Their catches were better than from shore and soon a boat became part of their natural fishing equipment. With a boat and a motor an angler could work a far greater area of water and he could parallel the shoreline thus working a whole trough from one end to the other. These troughs were often shaped like an elongated football and when fishing from shore the surf fisherman could get only one short run across the hole on each cast thereby never really getting a chance to fish from one end of a ledge to the other.

However, the real beginning of the revolution in striper fishing began the day one of the boat anglers took some big bass on pieces of dead mackerel. Others followed and this too became the accepted bait, but one day there were some live mackerel in close to shore and the bass went wild chasing them about. The fish could be observed coming right to the top and giving chase to the mackerel. Finally one of the anglers dropped a diamond jig overboard and took a mackerel. While the fish was still in the water he stuck a hook in its back and then let the fish have a free line to run among the sandbars. This mackerel was securely connected to his striper rod and he was amazed for the bait didn't get 30 feet from the boat when a thirty pound bass was there to give chase. The big striper hit that mackerel like it was the best dinner anyone ever offered it. This was the revolution in striper fishing.

This was a complete revolution too for the anglers soon learned they had chanced upon live-lining the best way yet discovered to take the prize stripers. Big fish that for years had passed by all the baits they offered would come dashing after the mackerel and where, at one time, a 30 pound striper was considered an exceptionally big fish they now became a regularity. David Webb estimates that in the area from Race Point to Nauset Beach during one year at least 5,000 fish over 40 pounds were taken and virtually all of them by live-lining.

The live mackerel fishing has its drawbacks too and one of the serious ones is getting the mackerel and keeping them alive. Out at Race Point it generally means the anglers must head offshore ¾ of a mile just past the offshore lobster traps and there, with a light spinning rod, jig for them. Catching them can sometimes be a problem but keeping them alive is always a serious problem for no fish dies faster out of water than a mackerel. What the anglers must do is catch them and immediately drop them into drums filled with fresh seawater. Even there the problem doesn't end for many mackerel just roll over and die if the water isn't kept absolutely fresh. On the trip back from offshore it means an angler has to stop at least 2 or 3 times to change the water so that they stay alive. Some anglers have taken to ripping their boats apart so that they can get a baitwell with fast circulating water in order to keep the mackerel better.

Once the angler gets back into striper water on the inside of the bars he stops his boat. Then he reaches down and takes a mackerel, and as fast as he can he inserts a big 6/0 to 9/0 hook in the back of the fish just behind the head. Moving quickly he puts the live bait in the ocean. The mackerel will start swimming along the water running parallel to the shore and running the whole length of the bar. The big stripers down there will come up and really chase that mackerel—these were the fish that for years couldn't be budged. If there are no takers for the mackerel the bait is given a free line to run down about 300 feet before it is slowly worked back to the boat again.

It is a constant source of amazement to these anglers that this same mackerel which so quickly dies out of water will be such a sturdy strong baitfish in water. If the mackerel gets into the ocean alive, it can be on a hook for over a half hour being worked through the holes and when it comes back to the boat it will be just as fresh as when it was first caught. Other baitfish have been tried including herring, sardines and pollack. Either the baitfish will have poor lasting power on a hook or like the pollack it will have a tendency to simply sink to the bottom and sulk, thus not attracting the bass. All the other available baitfish have proven themselves inferior to mackerel.

When one of the big stripers go after the mackerel the angler lets the bait run until the striper catches it and swallows the bait. Then the angler sets the hook by lifting the rod. His drag will be pre-set at approximately 10 pounds of pressure and his reel will now be snapped into gear. The hooked fish will need no one to tell him he is in trouble and he will begin to run. David Webb says, "You can tell the moment a fish is on if it is a big one. A bull striper has that extra strength and weight that makes him very difficult to turn when he starts running." The way the fish is turned is that he runs against the drag and the angler begins applying thumb pressure against the line on the reel. Some anglers will apply the pressure against the spool, but both Dave and Rosa Webb squeeze the line. This can give an angler an awfully hot blistery thumb therefore he must make sure that all his line is wet for this protects against the "hot thumb."

Pressure is added and eventually the fish is turned and is facing the angler. He may be almost 150 yards away from the boat and now he must be worked in. Dave says, "It doesn't matter whether the angler is on shore or in a boat, the way to bring a big fish in is by pumping and reeling him in. If I'm standing in the surf I put the rod butt between my legs and pump and reel to open the fishes mouth. This is done exactly the same way deep-sea anglers do it. In a boat it is the same pumping and reeling that brings them in." David Webb is a big 6 footer who can really move his fish with authority, but his wife Rosa, a pretty feminine girl, also agrees that man or girl this is the only way to bring the big stripers to gaff.

"The strange thing about stripers," says David Webb, "is that the biggest ones are not the best fighters. If a fish over fifty pounds takes your line you get one real hard run out of him, but after you turn him and begin pumping and reeling you soon notice that about half way in the fish will turn belly up and get dragged in. Get a fish about thirty pounds and you will have to fight him every inch of the way. The smaller ones have more lasting power and during a fight they may take three or four hard runs and really make an angler work. The very big fish will be dead when they are gaffed, but the smaller ones will still be full of fight. It seems among stripers the bigger the fish the faster he tires."

Before the advent of the live-lining many good anglers would go through life without ever catching a single fish in excess of 50 pounds. The Webb's luckily had a few to their credit and as of today David and Rosa Webb have taken over a dozen fish that weighed in excess of the half century mark.

Both of the Webb's biggest fish came in 1960 while fishing with mackerel. On August 14th of that year they were out in their boat. After having diligently caught their mackerel they began fishing. Suddenly Rosa's rod doubled over and a fish took off. She lifted her rod up and applied her thumb to the reel gradually slowing and turning the fish. Then the fifteen minute battle to bring it in and finally landing and boarding a big bass that was later to weigh in at 53½ pounds. Out went another mackerel and down into the water he went running along the drops. They worked the fish for a while when Rosa's rod doubled over again and she struck her fish. This one ran even harder and took out over 100 yards of her line. "I thought he was going to run my 150 yards of line right off the reel," she says, "but eventually I turned him." Then she pumped and reeled and worked hard on him until he turned belly up with the fight out of him. "This is a big one," she said to her husband when they had him at the side of the boat. They stuck the gaff in the fish and pulled him into the boat without further trouble. Both of them could see this was a really big fish and as soon as they were ashore someone suggested weighing it for a possible record. The fish was weighed in and on the beach scales weighed slightly over 70 pounds. You can imagine the excitement—a 70 pound fish—that would make it the second largest striper ever taken, bigger than Ralph Gray's number 2 fish which was 68 pounds, 5 ounces and certainly beating out her friendly rival Kay Townsend's biggest fish of 63½ pounds which had been taken earlier that day.

Then it was a drive to the official weighing station where the big fish was again placed on the scales. Here it weighed 64½ pounds showing that the beach scale was over 5 pounds off. This definitely took the fish out of the category of the second biggest fish ever, but it still was quite a record fish. Rosa cut a section of her line off and made arrangements to register the fish in the International Game Fish Association records. They took pictures and sent a sample of their 36 pound line along with the papers. When all the reports were finally in they found this line which they had bought at a tackle show wasn't 36 pound test nylon at all, but was 30 pound test. Thus the striper went into the records as the largest striper taken by women on 30 pound test line, the largest striper taken by both men and women anglers on 30 pound test line, and the largest striper ever taken by a woman—quite a fish even if it didn't weigh 70 pounds.

Many men would say David Webb was in kind of a fix then but exactly one week later he had a big strike. "Got one" he said, "check the time this is a good one." The fish ran hard and heavy but he turned it and fought it in. About half way back the fish turned belly up and the rest of the way it was dead weight. He brought it into the boat and checking the time it had taken exactly 13 minutes to boat. As the fish lay in the boat the anglers agreed it looked even bigger than Rosa's of the week before. When it was officially weighed the striper was exactly 64½ pounds—tying his wife's fish exactly. This striped bass was taken on line that was really 36 pound test so that its only distinction is that it is tied with his wife's fish and the fish of still another angler as the 13th largest striper ever taken up to that time.

Although the Webbs and other anglers have had phenomenal success with live-lining mackerel one can easily tell just by talking to them that there exists a real yearning to go back to the beach to fish. Rosa Webb says that on some night she is glad to see the ocean riled up, for then they will fish the surf and won't take the boat out. The Webb's boat is seaworthy but their fishing is strictly pleasure fishing so that they sensibly do not take unnecessary chances. When they fish from the beach it is just like old times with them and they love every minute of it. David Webb says, "If we could catch two fish a night I'd get rid of the boat." But the catch results are so superior in a boat that this fishing is now part of the repertoire for almost all anglers. Still they languidly remember the good times on the beach such as the time of the blitz in 1956 when in one night they took so many big stripers they could hardly squeeze them into their buggy.

One of the times the anglers enjoy the most is when a run of small stripers is on along the beach. This gives them a chance to forget the boat and whip out their light spinning rods and then using 8 and 10 pound test monofilament line they attack the surf. Today the favorite plugs for this kind of fishing are long thin plugs which are retrieved through the water at an almost break neck speed. The plugs most of the anglers are finding very successful are Stan Gibb's Pencil Poppers. These are long and thin and should be retrieved very swiftly so that the front jumps out of the water just like a speedboat. The front of the plug will wobble back and forth and the bass come up and really smash at this plug. The plugs are getting longer and thinner each year and the retrieve faster—now with the higher gear ratio spinning reels it means an even faster retrieve is possible.

Some of the striper anglers are making an effort to get maximum results from the beach. It has always been that one section of a beach will be catching fish while possibly as little as a few hundred yards away they won't get a nibble. Thus many of the anglers that fish in clubs are now installing radios in their buggies and some are even taking to using walkie talkies. The theory being that when some anglers get fish they announce over the radio, "Hea there hitting here." Everyone then jumps into his buggy and hurries to that spot. The Webbs don't have much faith in this process for there is no greater luxury than to have a hole to oneself where the fish are hitting. Part of the joy of fishing is coming back and asking the others, "What's wrong with you anyway? Why can't you get fish? Want lessons?"

Striper anglers have always been an independent breed of fishermen and one rule of the beach is if you see someone catching fish in a particular spot you are free to move right up next to him and take your share. This sometimes resulted in flared tempers and crossed lines, but it was part of the rules of surf fishing. Dave Webb remembers one night when one of his friends was fishing light tackle and he hit into something big that bullied him all over the beach. Dave said, "Other anglers won't get out of the way for you either if they have any chance to get a fish for themselves. This angler spent the next hour ducking over and under dozens of lines as the fish took him a half a mile upbeach. He lost it just before he could land it so that he quickly went back and took out the sturdier tackle, for on a crowded beach control of a fish is very important."

David Webb feels the radio cooperation will work something like this. The angler will find a beach where they are hitting and he soon will forget all about his radio until he has enough fish at which time he might remember to call to tell the others to tell them the fish had been hitting pretty good, but they seemed to have stopped about a half an hour ago.

There is one point David and Rosa Webb feel strongly about, just as do the members of the many New England striper fishing clubs. The International Game Fish Association, which keeps the official records of salt water catches, has a rule which says "In a claim for an IGFA record, the use of a plug is permissible only if not more than two single hooks are attached to the plug." The striper anglers feel this rule is unfair when applied to striper fishing for virtually all bass plugs are made with two sets of treble hooks and they feel it is much harder and sportier to get a fish on a plug than by any other method. Striper anglers say the rule should be amended to permit the use of two sets of treble hooks on a plug.

Another rule they feel might be worthwhile changing is the rule against the use of wire line. When striper anglers use it they only use it to get their baits to the bottom for there has never been a better sinker invented. The line offers no other advantage and it seems strange to penalize an angler for this. It is unfair that the 73 pound striper taken by Charles E. Cinto at Cuttyhunk, Massachusetts on June 16, 1967 was disqualified from International Game Fish Association Records because excess wire line was used.

David and Rosa Webb are certain that there are stripers in excess of the 73 pound world record and Mr. Cinto's unrecognized fish on the New England shoreline every year. They feel just as certain that the live-lining way of fishing can take one of these super lunkers and they hope against hope it will be one of them that takes this fish. Yet, if they take it or if they do not take it, one thing is certain that this fishing couple will be out there on the Cape Cod beach trying for the fish because this is the sport they love and for them there is no finer place than life on the beach.

7. CHANNEL BASS FISHING WITH BILL DILLON

"The greatest thrill I get fishing is when I am down on the Hatteras beach at night and slug it out with a big 40 to 50 pound channel bass in a fight that will crackle with excitement for a half hour and more," says angler Bill Dillon.

Mr. William Dillon moved to Buxton on Hatteras Island in 1950 and started the Outer Banks Motel which has become a meeting place for sports fishermen. Bill says, "When I moved to Buxton I actually knew very little about channel bass except the fact they had the reputation of being the toughest fighting surf fish. I started fishing for them the first week I was here. Going down to the surf I hit into a couple of them, but broke off line after line and couldn't hold a single fish of any size. That cured me of light tackle and I went down and got myself some heavy duty surf equipment. Then I began to bring in a few fish. Through the years I found that 36 pound test line wound on a Penn Squidder Reel and backed up on a Harnell Surf Rod suited my fishing just fine. I found this tackle was sufficiently strong to hold the biggest and most rugged fish in even the strongest tides and currents while I feel it is still flexible enough to be sporty."

Bill Dillon thinks channel bass are the finest surf fish in the country. He points out that for Southern anglers from Maryland to Florida on the Atlantic coast, and in the Gulf from Florida to Texas think the channel bass is the most important inshore fish. Still inspite of the channel bass wide distribution and importance to anglers, it is a neglected fish for few, if any, studies were ever made and little is known of its migratory habits.

Bill, who knows these fish from years of sport and study, explains that a channel bass is not a fast sleek swimming fish, but a coarse fish that is a sports fish because it has tremendous strength and stamina. He goes on to explain that a channel bass crushes any crab that it decides on for dinner, and it crushes oyster shells in its vice like jaws to the dismay of the oystermen everywhere. When this fish is on a line it will make sustained runs that really put strain on a line. Although angler Bill Dillon loves light tackle fishing, he simply does not think it is suited for big drum over 40 pounds. He says, "I use light salt water spinning rods when I go for puppy drum, those fish that weight 5 pounds or less, and have wonderful sport."

This expert tells anglers that the best time to surf fish for the giant 40 to 60 pounders from the Virginia, North Carolina and South Carolina beaches is in the fall. At Hatteras Island, which he considers the best spot for channel bass fishing, the season begins about the 15th of October. Other spots along the coast will have the season vary by only a few weeks. He says, "The prime season at Hatteras extends right on through November and into December for as long as the weather holds up. This is the time of year for the angler who wants to fish for trophy sized fish. Night after night there will be runs of bull bass in the surf, and by fishing the tides correctly an angler will regularly hit into 2 or 3 big bull bass a night."

There is also a run of fish at the Outer Banks in the springtime beginning about April 15th and extending to May 15th, but Bill warns this run does not compare to the fall run in the number of fish available to surf anglers. He says, "One night an angler may get 1 or 2 good sized fish but then the next 2 or 3 nights nothing at all will be taken as the fish stay offshore outside the reach of the surf angler. Throughout the spring the fish are offshore and come into the surf only on occasions. The anglers here who want fish in the spring do best in a boat chartering with one of the local captains because he then reaches those fish 150 to 400 yards oflshore. They also hook some nice ones from the piers here in North Carolina and up at Virginia Beach during the spring but unfortunately surf fishing is spotty.

"As soon as warm weather sets in channel bass get scarcer and scarcer for the surf anglers until by the middle of May they will be completely gone. The boat anglers fishing out of Oregon Inlet, Hatteras or Ocracoke will continue taking these fish in the ocean right through May, but their fishing drops off too. Right at this time bluefish and cobia will start inshore, while dolphin, white marlin and gigantic blue marlin will be caught offshore. After June there will still be some bass taken in the bay but they are usually puppy drum and other fishing will have pushed this sport into the background.

"In the fall the first signs of channel bass picking up will be when the boats start bringing them in usually about the middle of September. Gradually the fish will begin working into the surf until about October 15th when they will be there in force."

This expert advises, "Surf fishing for channel bass is primarily night fishing, as the fish come closer to the shoreline at night than during the days. They don't come in close during the day because they are very light shy. I had one experience that clearly showed me just how light shy these fish really are. I had hooked into a big one which I battled and was finally bringing it into the surf to gaff. Then directly behind me on the beach a car headlight turned on and shone right on my fish in the surf. That fish just went beserk on me—twisting and running diving for the deep water ripping line from my reel. I had to let it run and then began working the fish in again. After a long struggle I got the bass to the beach and wouldn't you know it but that car's headlights went on again. Once more the fish took off and I let him go because there isn't much you can do when a big one decides to run. The fish settled in deep water and I began all over again. That bass still had plenty of fight left, showing me the tremendous strength and stamina they have, but finally I got him through the surf, gaffed him and dragged the big bull bass to the beach without further interference. I'm sure I would have had that fish the first time if that light hadn't gone on—it really showed how sensitive they are to light."

Mr. Dillon advises that since surf fishing takes place at night, the angler should get down to the beach on the day before and study the water. He says, "I look for changes in the surf and locate where the dropoffs are and mark the spots mentally. I like to do my fishing right along the dropoffs and in channels for this is where the fish will be congregated. The beaches at Hatteras are always changing so even the regulars like us have to constantly recheck the beaches because we want to fish the likely spots and don't want to waste time in shallow water.

"Possibly the most important item in channel bass fishing is to make certain the tides are right for even at the height of the fall season, fishing will be poor at the wrong times of the tide. I arrange to begin fishing just about 1 hour before the high tide and I only stay until 1 or 2 hours after the tide has begun to recede. How long I stay of course, depends upon how the fish continue hitting, but one thing is certain if they stop hitting between 1 and 2 hours after the tide begins receeding, the chances are that that is the end of fishing for the night—except of course for strays which I don't consider worth waiting for. If I'm busy at my motel and I can get away only for an hour or so I make sure it is at the point of the absolute high tide—this is the best time to fish because the fish will be out over the flood bank and busy searching food.

"Channel bass have mouths that are a combination nut cracker and bottle opener. They chop an oyster or clam in two with one chop of their tremendously strong jaws and a crab doesn't stand a chance when a fish descends on one. Many anglers use crabs as baits and often they crush the crab shell thinking this helps the fish to swallow the meat. It is helpful to crush the shell because the juices of the crab will seep out and help attract fish, but shells never bother these fish.

"I have used crabs, clams, and artificials for baits, but through the years I found a piece of cut fish does as well as any other bait I ever tried. Whenever possible I get a piece of mullet and cut off about a 3-inch square piece which I put on a 7/0 or 8/0 hook. When I can't get mullet and I use one of the other available fish chunks it really has no noticeable effect. The one thing about channel bass is that they are hogs and will literally eat any and everything in sight. I know some that have been pulled up with bottles, pieces of steel, rocks and all kinds of things in their stomach. I've come to the conclusion that virtually any kind of bait will do. The important thing in channel bass fishing is not baits, but proper timing of season and tides and getting the baits out to the hotspots. Be in the right spot at the right time and any kind of bait will get one to hit. When a bull bass moves along the bottom searching food he will take the first edible looking thing.

"Often the fish will come up to the bait and merely grab it really just mouthing the bait. The angler must give the fish time. When I feel a fish on my bait I wait. I've had fish that have pushed the bait 25 feet and more never really taking it. The only thing for the angler to do is to wait patiently. Sometimes the fish will mouth the bait and run 5 to 10 yards with it only to spit it out again. Beginning anglers often make the mistake of striking too soon and ripping the line from the fishes mouth. Other times when they strike too soon they get a weakly hooked fish they later lose in the fight. The best advice I can give an angler is to wait—it will pay off.

"With this fish even if he should feel a hook while he fools with a bait it will not deter him from taking the bait and it will not deter him from finishing the meal. A channel bass has a mouth that is used to the sharp edges of oyster and crab shells therefore the taste of the metal point of a hook does not bother the fish. This big strong fish must be given time but when I feel he really has the bait I strike my line hard. I lift my big surf rod high over my shoulder to set the hook deeply in the tough mouth. The fight ahead is going to be a long hard one and I want my hook set good because when I hook a fish I want to catch him. No angler need ever concern himself about striking too hard with these fish simply rear back and let him have it—if he is hooked then he will be on to stay."

Once the fish is on he begins fighting immediately. Bill Dillon claims, "They are pier six sluggers! A big bass will run hard out to sea along the bottom and will shake his head angrily. If there are any sharp rocks or ledges around you can bet 10 to 1 that he will head right there where he will scrape repeatedly along the bottom in an effort to cut the line. They never hurt themselves but they can sure cut up a line that way. I always check the last 50 feet of the line after each trip because sometimes it gets frayed and dangerously understrength from scraping.

"Whenever I begin a fight with a big bass I immediately try to show the fish who is boss and right from the start I put heavy pressure on the fish. My drag is preset at 8 to 10 pounds and when the fish wants line he has to work for it. When he takes off on a run of course I give him all the line he wants but he will be working against the drag all the way. The moment the fish stops running I begin to reel in trying to lead him to the beach. I reel hard and it's straining work because the fish will resist with all his power and strength. Still some of them will suddenly follow the line right in and can be taken with comparatively little trouble. These fish have become confused and are really stolen, but most of the time it will be a knock down no holds barred pier six brawl with anything over 30 pounds. It generally takes me 30 minutes to an hour with a bull of this size.

"Some battles really get exciting and during a fight the fish often run parallel to the beach and then I have to take off along the beach trying to follow their run. By following them I can shorten up on the amount of line I have out which cuts down drag on the line and allows me to put more direct pressure on the fish. Still it is never easy to go stumbling along in the dark in what is often a heavy surf. I always get sprayed and on more occasions than I can remember I've slipped and ended up thoroughly soaked in the cold night ocean. Still when you are after a fish you can't stop. I just get up and continue going after the fish. Generally I'm properly dressed with waterproof clothes and I generally don't feel uncomfortable until after the fish is landed.

"If a fish thinks it is in control of the situation it seems to pick up momentum in its battle and that is why I stress putting maximum pressure on a fish to show it who is in control. They are not easy to move either and I've taken more than one angler out with me who after an hour or two of fighting simply had enough and cut the fish off. Most anglers, though, will fight one in no matter how long or hard the fight may be, but after that they simply slip up on the beach with their prize and they have had enough.

'One thing about channel bass is that they really give an angler a workout from hookup to the time they are beached. Any angler that gets two big ones in a night knows he has done some fishing and if he is not used to it he will have some pretty angry muscles the next morning."

Angler Bill Dillon sums up channel bass fishing by saying "The important thing in this fishing isn't the choice of baits or finesse in fishing. My advice for the angler who wants big ones is to get on a good beach at night during high tide in the height of the surf season and then simply cast a piece of fish out to a drop-off and wait. When the angler has battled and taken a 30 to 60 pound bull bass he will agree with me that this is the finest sports fishing there is." And there isn't a surf angler from Texas to Virginia who won't agree.

Jimmy Holt displays a fine catch of Kentucky Lake Bass.

Surf anglers waiting for the tide so they can head down to the beach for channel bass.

On a typical Catskill trout stream such as this one, Harry Darbee will walk along the shore until he sees signs of rising fish and will then fish there.

A typical 16-pound striped bass of the kind regularly taken surf fishing.

A 26-foot Pacemaker Sport Fisherman heads out to open water to do a little white marlin trolling.

A four-pound largemouth bass.

This former world record blue marlin of John Battles taken in the Virgin Islands July 26, 1964 was the fish all anglers hoped to beat. (U.S. Virgin Islands Official Photo.)

8. MARLIN FISHING WITH DONALD LEEK

Donald Leek, a young angler, is recognized by his contemporaries as one of the fastest up and coming bill fishing experts in the country. Don has already acted as chairman in such major tournaments as the Hatteras International Blue Marlin Tournament, The Atlantic City White Marlin Tournament, The Ocean City Tournament and has served on the board for The Bimini Tournament and the Palm Beach Sailfish Tournament. Mr. Leek comes from a long line of seafaring families who have been boat builders for seven generations and he is currently President of Alglass Corporation a subsidiary of C. P. Leek and Sons, Inc., maker of the complete line of Pacemaker sportsfishing and pleasure boats.

Don Leek began billfishing over a decade ago and since then has accelerated this quest for the big fish continually. He caught his first white marlin and fell in love with this sportsfishing. Since then he has caught an estimated 200 white marlin. Don says, "I think white marlin are the finest sportsfish available to anglers and certainly the best billfish as they are so readily accessible from so many places along the Atlantic coast." Then he points out that white marlin go up to 175 pounds and says, "Best of all, no matter what size they are they all fight like hell."

Mr. Leek, like most good anglers has developed his own style of fishing for the whites. He says, "White marlin are not really big fish, the average size being only about 60 pounds. That means, if you want sport, it's best to stick to somewhat light tackle. I generally stay with 20 or 30 pound class outfits. Here I get ample control of a fish and I get great sport."

He feels one of the real crimes of sportsfishing is the anglers who get white marlin on ultra heavy duty tackle. Too often a white will be taken while an angler is fishing for blue marlin and then the smaller fish almost gets wenched in. When Don hears of an angler berating a white, it really gets him because he knows if that same angler fought this fish on light 20 or 30 pound class tackle he would be glowing of the fish's leaps, runs acrobatics and its tremendous tenacious spirit.

Balanced tackle of 20 or 30 pound class is what Mr. Leek considers best for this fishing. He thinks that if an angler were an absolute beginner then possibly a 50 pound class outfit could be tolerated and he points out many of the charter boats use this class tackle simply because they get so many beginners. However, any experienced fisherman will want a 30 pound class rod and line. He says, "I still do much of my fishing with a 30 pound class rod and a 4/0 Penn or Fin-Nor Reel. My line is either dacron or monofilament of 30 pound test. There is plenty of challenge here while at the same time the tackle is light enough to enjoy the spectacular fighting qualities of the average size white marlin of 50 or 60 pounds.

"Other times," he says, "I use a balanced 20 pound class outfit. Then, I really have fireworks with every white I hook." He points out that as far as he is concerned he has found fishing with 10 or 12 pound class outfits is purely stunt fishing. With tackle this light the angler has absolutely no control of a fish and he must depend entirely on his captain's ability to keep chasing the fish all over the ocean. He explains, "I once had what must have been a 100 pound white marlin on a 12 pound class outfit and for 3 hours we chased that fish up and down the Maryland coast. I finally cut the line in disgust. The captain could have maneuvered the boat in close and I could have guided the fish alongside but we would have had to throw a gaff into a fresh fish. I couldn't honestly have said that I caught that fish because I didn't beat him. This just isn't fishing in my book."

Once out in marlin waters the lines go out and he begins the hunt for the fish—trolling miles of ocean, criss crossing back and forth over what they feel are the hotspots. They search the ocean looking for tailing fish that are on the surface while their baits are out. They will troll moving 4 to 6 knots an hour and a days fishing generally calls for 10 hours on the water with the baits tended and watched almost constantly.

While talking about white marlin trolling Don says, "Contrary to popular belief, white marlin are not boat shy and they will come right in close to the boat. I fish only 3 lines, 2 off the outriggers and one flat. Our flat line is set up so that the bait rides no more than 35 feet behind the boat. The two lines off the outrigger will be back another 15 feet. Fishing in close and only fishing 3 lines off the back makes it so we almost never get a tangle—even on the windiest and roughest days.

"Most boats will fish their hooks back somewhere between 50 and 100 feet, but I found this isn't necessary as it has no effect on the number of strikes, while the shorter lines create fishing excitement. When a fish looms up behind the bait you're right on top of the action. It makes for some of the most exciting moments in the sport and sometimes when a fish jumps you feel like he is going to leap right into the boat."

When the lines are out they will put a Cerant Teaser running ten feet behind the boat. Mr. Leek has seen lots of fish close in for the teaser, but since they are hookless and are kept there only as an added attraction the mate will pull it right in.

Don Leek admits, "I'm a little bit of a stickler on baits. I have certain preferences and whenever I can get them my favorite is a small fresh squid only about 4 to 6 inches long. We take these and run a 5/0 hook through them and then sew them to the hook. There isn't a white marlin in the ocean that can resist this bait when they are in a feeding mood. The only problem I find with squid baits is getting them, as I have to find a commercial fisherman that has some fresh ones available."

Another bait he has very good luck with is a ballyhoo, which is a small baitfish that doesn't look too different from a baby marlin. This fish has a bill just like the bigger billfish specie. One trouble with these is that they get water logged quite easily when they aren't perfectly fresh. When this happens they put a plastic skirt over the bait which helps the whole thing stay together. The skirt doesn't have any effect on the number of strikes the bait gets. Don recalls one afternoon using some of the most overripe baits he ever had occasion to fish he had at least six strikes.

A silver mullet is still another bait that brings him good results. These can be purchased frozen, or still better he likes them fresh. They are flown up from Florida and are generally available at many of the sportsfishing centers. The mullet is sewn onto a 5/0 or 6/0 Mustad hook after it is gutted. The hook is inserted in the mouth and out the stomach cavity which is then stitched together.

"I have used a variety of other baits including mackerel, Spanish mackerel, bluefish and even pieces of cut tuna. I've tried artificial baits too but I just don't go for them. My best luck has been with squid, ballyhoo and mullet in that order."

Sometimes when trolling, he will place a ½ to a 1 ounce weight right in front of the bait. This helps keep the bait in the water and helps it to swim in a realistic manner.

There was a time when Don Leek fished by the book in that his lines were 50 to 100 feet behind the boat and then as soon as a fish tapped that bait he would drop the bait back in the traditional way of big game fishing. Then, in the accepted method he would continue dropping back further and further, sometimes so that his line might be out 150 feet back in theory that the marlin gets the idea that it injured the bait on the first hit and it then comes back to devour the stricken bait. Don is convinced he has a better way and now instead of dropping back on the sight of a fish behind his bait he takes a couple of cranks on the reel and sometimes lifts the rodtip actually taking the bait away from the fish.

"One day the marlin were out there but they were spooky and never really took a bait. I missed about four that had come right up to my bait and I was disgusted. When another one appeared I lifted my rodtip to see what would happen. To my surprise the fish came right at the bait and struck it harder than I'd ever had a white marlin strike. After the strike, that fish leaped right out of the water. Four times in a row he jumped clean up and then I had a great battle. It was a solidly hooked fish and I got him."

Don doesn't drop back anymore. He explains, "When a fish hits one of the baits riding from the outrigger and knocks it off of there, the angler has an automatic dropback. This is plenty for if the white hasn't struck a second time by the time the slack has run out he isn't going to. I then quickly take a crank or two on the reel and more often than not this helps induce that big hit.

"Reeling in instead of dropping back worked wonders for me and it gradually developed into my own style of fishing. I think by pulling the bait away from a marlin it stirs his natural instinct as a hunter of food. Under natural conditions if the marlin goes at a bait, even an injured baitfish would try to escape and the big fish will have to lunge harder and swifter at it. I think my taking a crank on the reel duplicates this and stirs the marlin's natural instinct to strike hard before the bait escapes.

"I have pulled the bait away from a marlin three, four and even five times. This can really infuriate some of the fish. At times you can lead them to within 10 feet of the boat. I have seen them get so excited over missing the bait they become oblivious of anything else around. And best of all when they do hit they hit hard and you're really in for some close in fighting with a highly angered fresh strong marlin. At times they blast out of the water like shots and really stir up the ocean."

Fighting a white marlin, Don Leek explains, is a terribly exciting thing. Out there the angler fights a fish with the heart of a lion coupled with tremendous strength all packed into a beautifully streamlined body. Still the angler has the odds with him for he controls the rod, reel and line. He has a drag which should be set about 10 pounds and that means that all the while the fish is on the hook he will have to drag 10 pounds of weight with him. This of course tires the fish and Don wonders how they manage to fight as long and as hard as they do.

Don Leek fought his first few white marlin sitting in a fighting chair, but now he simply places the rod in a belt and fights the fish standing up. Some of the smaller whites will be fought by simply holding the rod and reeling at the right times. He explains it doesn't take brute strength to overpower a fish. It is more a matter of applying pressure at the right times. These fish love acrobatics and when they are jumping or running the angler should simply drop the rod tip and let the fish tire itself out. The all important thing, of course, is to keep slack out of the line for slack lines lead to ripped hooks and popped lines. Once the fish stops running Don pumps the rod to open the fishes mouth and then he drops the rod tip as he reels in line. Time and time again—lift the rod, open the fishes mouth—drop the rod tip reeling it down until the fish is exhausted and can be led to the side of the boat.

Today, he can beat an averaged size white marlin using 30 pound tackle in 10 minutes or less and he has done it in 5 minutes time from hookup. Don insists that a fish be thoroughly worn out before it is brought to the boat as he will never boat a fresh fish.

When the fish is thoroughly spent, it is brought alongside. Then sometimes Don or the mate reach down with a gloved hand, grab the bill and pull the fish up over the railing. Don says, "I take many guests out and very often the fish they catch will be their first one. They generally want it mounted and I do not blame them one bit for wanting the trophy. With a gloved hand I then reach down and grab the bill, and with one motion pull the fish over the side. We generally have a club handy to quiet it and stop it from jumping about too much.

"The fish I have on myself will only be lifted up to the rail and then we quickly put a bill tag on him. The mate then cuts the leader with a wire cutter to snip off the hook and the fish drops back into the water. For a few seconds it will just sit there not realizing it is free, but then with a little movement he will swim a short way, then move a little more like he were testing to see if he is really free. Then the fish simply dives out of sight. It is always good to see a fish dive down because that fish will be okay and the sport will continue.

"We leave the hook in the fish's mouth because we know that in salt water, it doesn't last long and will disintegrate. It never hurts the fish."

Don Leek explains that white marlin spread themselves over a vast area of the Atlantic coast and any angler willing to take a long boatride could probably catch some from virtually any port from Florida to Massachusetts. The fish come out of their wintering areas of the Caribbean and the Bahamas in the beginning of May and start to migrate North generally following the Gulf Stream. They arrive off the coast of the Carolinas and in late May and then by June the fish are off Virginia. The big migration will continue North and tremendous amounts of fish will settle in the fecund waters of Ocean City, Maryland by the end of June, staying there through July and August. Others will spread themselves out along New Jersey, Long Island and Southern New England. Each area will have vast amounts of marlin in their big game fishing grounds.

For the angler who wants to take a real crack at white marlin fishing, Don feels the most important item is to fish one of the established hotspots during the height of the season. He feels that probably the best single spot on the Atlantic coast would be Ocean City, Maryland during the summer months. If the angler puts himself into the hands of a good captain and fishes Ocean City waters the chances are best that he will get his fish. One point that makes Ocean City unique is that there are no less than five white marlin hotspots easily accessible from this port.

Mr. Leek loves to fish Ocean City and explains that it has

been the white marlin capitol for years. It began in 1933 when a hurricane blew a hole in Assateague Island off the coast of Maryland. This made an inlet and an excellent small boat harbor. It didn't take long for some sportsfishing boats to venture out and explore the offshore ocean to see just what fishing was available. Mr. Paul Townsend in 1934 was the first to say it looked like there was a likely billfish feeding shoal some 22 miles Southwest of the new Ocean City Inlet ana that year the first captures were made confirming his belief. This shoal was soon labeled Jack Spot and it was a tremendously exciting find as this location was miles North of any known marlin waters. Jack Spot has been fished ever since and it traditionally produces handsomely during the summer months when the fish get over the shoal to feed. Today, the major complaint against this spot is the tremendous fishing pressure it undergoes every year for probably no where else in the world has one billfishing ground been fished so relentlessly.

Other fishing areas were discovered by boats fishing out of Ocean City and by oceanographers. Chief among these are the 3 canyons located within fishing distance of the port. These canyons, Norfolk, Baltimore and Wilmington Canyons are steep walls along the continental shelf where billfish congregate to feed on the smaller fish that stay in the area.

Early in the season, generally about June 15th to 30th, depending on the weather the fish first appear in number off Norfolk Canyon which is a 73 mile run 175° out of Ocean City. Another excellent producing canyon is Baltimore Canyon, a run of 59 nautical miles 105° from Ocean City. The third canyon fished extensively is Wilmington Canyon which is 76 miles 90°. Wilmington Canyon is also fished by boats of Redoubt Beach as well as boats coming from Southern New Jersey.

The canyons generally offer the best fishing when the water is clear and settled. They generally offer poor fishing after large storms that stir up the water and make poor visibility. When this occurs the fish stay down in the depths and won't rise to the anglers baits. However, when the fish are hitting at the canyons the angler may well hit into school tuna, sharks or just about anything in the ocean, but best of all he could have several marlin hits in one day. Mr. Leek has had over a dozen hits on a few occasions.

Whenever Don Leek's boat fishes a canyon they make it a point to fish along the edges where the water is 40 to 50 fathoms deep. This is generally the best depth for fishing as the baitfish seem to congregate at the edges. When the marlin are in water of this depth they are feeding and readily attack a bait. "I have raised as many as 13 fish in a day at Delaware Canyon just moving about the edges of the canyon."

Out of Ocean City there is another possibility and some private owners have been heading out to fish the edges of the Gulf Stream. This is a long haul and it isn't done unless the angler has a boat at his command that is seaworthy and can do at least 18 to 20 knots. Also Don explains the boat should have good living quarters as the angler will do at least 7 hours of boat-riding just to get out and back.

Donald Leek, the professional boatbuilder, gives this advice to anglers who intend to extensively fish big game. Their boat should be at least 40 to 45 feet in length as big-game angling often means long offshore trips and the big boat rides much better when the sea gets rough. He suggests diesel power as upkeep and fuel expenses will be drastically cut. Don, whose favorite among the boats his family makes are the sportsfishing models, feels that a serious marlin angler should have a flying bridge on his boat. The added visibility from that height increases a captain's ability to spot tailing fish and see the shadows of fish that may be just under the surface. One other item to have is a transom door, for it is far easier to pull a big fish through a door than over the side or up a gin pole.

In summing up Ocean City fishing, Mr. Leek says, "Ocean City during the summer, I think is probably the best spot an angler can go for white marlin. If the fisherman wants to charter there is always an ample supply of charter boats with some excellent skippers and crews and for boat owners there are good docking facilities and easily accessible fishing waters. Some years there are as many as 2,000 white marlin taken on boats fishing from Ocean City, therefore I feel it gives both the fisherman chartering and those using their own boat the best chance there is for a white marlin."

The waters of the whole Atlantic coast are Mr. Leek's own backyard and he tells about one relatively lightly fished place that now shows signs of becoming a white marlin hotspot—Virginia Beach. Up to now, limited docking facilities and a 4½ to 5 hour boat trip to the fishing grounds have stopped Virginia Beach development. However, Don explains that 2 hours of that running time have been spent getting out of the bay and along the coast to open water. The construction of the new Rudi Inlet cut this 2 hour coastal running time from the trip. This plus plans to greatly expand docking facilities causes Mr. Leek to say, "In the next ten years Virginia Beach will really appear on the billfishing map. It wouldn't surprise me at all if this turned out to be a white and blue marlin fishing ground of major importance."

Atlantic City is another fine spot for white marlin fishing. Anglers can fish the Hudson or Wilmington Canyons from here and during certain times of the summer they really catch them. He says, "Although my own boat is kept at Ocean City, we generally have a demonstrator here at Atlantic City as it is so close to Egg Harbor where we manufacture our boats. Just to show how good fishing gets here one day the party I took out raised 11 fish. We hooked 7 of them and boated 4, releasing them all. Another thing about Atlantic City is that it is convenient for so many anglers from New York or Philadelphia. There are ample charter boats here and it makes good fishing for both the boat owner or someone chartering."

Fishing tournaments are often a good reflection of the quality of fishing available and in 1962 and 1964 Atlantic City Tournament there were over 100 captures of white marlin brought to dock. This particular tournament doesn't give points for released fish so every fish was boated and docked. Mr. Leek stresses he personally would like to see the tournament make some kind of arrangements for releasing fish, but he appreciates the scope of the refereeing problem as there are always so many boats in the tournament. However, one good thing is that all the fish docked are used—some are given to institutions for food while others are sold in local restaurants. Most people do not realize that marlin are good eating fish—somewhat of the texture and taste of swordfish, but unfortunately a darker color. The meat can be smoked or broiled. In the Hawaiian Islands, Japan, the Caribbean and much of South and Central America, marlin is a much sought food fish.

To Americans, the marlin is primarily a sportfish and today both Don and his brother Jack Leek release just about every fish they catch. The only fish they keep are tournament fish or special fish—very large ones, etc. Other fish they keep will include those that die during the fight or those that get sharked. The Leek brothers thoughts about releasing fish are definite. They feel that after the angler has had all the thrill of capturing one of these marvelous high spirited fighting fish, and since he is not going to eat it then he should release it. This way there will always be an ample supply of game fish for the future. They always keep release packets aboard, and with scientists so anxious to enlist the aid of fishermen so that they can learn about the migrations of the fish and more about life in the ocean, it adds to the incentive. To date none of Don's or Jack's fish have been recaptured, but one day one of them could turn up in a strange spot thus giving science a new lesson on fish migration.

Don Leek goes on to tell about the good white marlin fishing that is available off Long Island and the Southern Coast of New England. This fishing is best in August, but there are captures from the middle of July on to early September. The hotspot is in the area of No Man's Land and in 1966 when Don was fishing out of Shinnecock he hooked into one. He had a 30 pound class outfit with monofilament line and that fish took full advantage. It was all over the ocean and simply would not respond to the rod the way a regular 70 to 90 pounder did. He knew it was big!

The fish then treated him to a spectacular half hour of leaps, runs and bulldogging until it finally tired. Don brought him in, but several times he broke away. However, it was a tired fish and finally the leader came over the side. Mate, Jim Baker broke out the gaff and put it into the fish's belly and hauled it aboard. Then Captain Carmey looked down, "Boss you might have yourself a world record there." They quit fishing because they were anxious to get to port and see if indeed they did have a world record for 30 pound test line. Don explains when you have a world record or near world record it is important to get in quickly for the fish can dry out and lose a pound or two which could well make the difference. At the dock it officially weighed in at 124 pounds which was just 6 pounds, 4 ounces under Leonard Henrix's 130 pound, 4 ounce world record fish for 30 pound test line taken in 1959 at Bimini in the Bahamas. Still Don realized it was a darn nice fish even if it didn't take all the marbles. There aren't many whites that come any bigger.

This catch and reports of other anglers catches led Don Leek to feel that there is a much larger concentration of white marlin off Long Island and Massachusetts than was ever anticipated. Anglers here simply do not center their fishing on this specie as they are more prone to concentrate on swordfish or tuna which calls for a completely different style of fishing.

When the first cold snap comes in September and the water temperatures start to dip, the white marlin will begin to disappear and start to move South. Generally, there will still be good marlin fishing right to the end of October off the North Carolina coast. The Hatteras Marlin club runs a big game tournament for members in October and in some years white and blue marlin catches will be quite good.

Hatteras and Oregon Inlet are both excellent white marlin producers, but Don Leek feels that for the whites Oregon Inlet would get the nod as the better place. This port brings in hundreds of whites every year which is amazing considering that there is only a fraction of the number of boats and anglers fishing as there is from the centers further North. This fact certainly proves what a fine white marlin fishing ground the waters off Oregon Inlet are. At Hatteras the thinking, the fishing, and the tackle is geared for blue marlin to the neglect of the whites. Then further South off Moorhead City, North Carolina, the anglers tend to fish exclusively for the big blue marlin because it takes 4 to 5 hours of boatriding to reach the fishing grounds.

There are plenty of marlin in the waters off South Carolina, Georgia and Northern Florida, but the trip out to the edges of the Gulf Stream is such a long boatride that fishing in these parts is more concentrated on the fish that come in closer to shore.

The Southern half of Florida has better billfishing because of the Gulf Stream, which is only a few miles from shore at West Palm Beach, Stuart or Miami. Whites are taken every year in almost every month of the year at these ports. A boat fishing out of Miami way back in 1938 produced the world's biggest white marlin—a 161 pounder. Several million white marlin have probably been taken all over the sportsfishing map since then, but none have been able to beat this fish. There have been several claims, but in each instance the fish turned out to be a blue marlin rather than a white. The white is generally identified by its somewhat whitish color on its sides and a rounded dorsal fin and a lateral line that runs down the side of the fish. Blue marlin, on the other hand, have more pointed dorsal fins and a more pointed anal fin while it does not have a lateral line, but instead many will tend to be striped vertically.

If an angler were to pick one spot in the world for marlin fishing, and he chose the Bahamas he couldn't help but choose well. This great fishing ground is probably best known for its blue marlin and tuna, but it also is in the International Game Fish Association record books for 12 pound, 20 pound, 30 pound and 130 pound test world record white marlin. The fish are in these waters all year long, but fishing concentration usually runs from about October until May. "The places I did most of my fishing in the Bahamas is at Bimini, Walker Cay and Chub Cay. An angler can take his pick for the best one as they are all superb producers. Fishing here is a real pleasure as the lines go out just 15 minutes out of port as the fish are within a few miles from shore."

Among other fine productive spots for white marlin where American anglers often fish are Puerto Rico and the Virgin Islands. They rank with the best. The fish are in these waters all year long but the best time for white marlin begins in March and extends through about the middle of June. The summer months of July and August are probably the slowest here for white marlin while April and May are the favorites.

Actually white marlin are found throughout the Caribbean and generally near a ledge next to a dropoff would be a likely spot for them. At one time Cuba ranked high as a white and blue marlin hotspot. "To me, it would seem that it would be a real angling adventure for an angler to try his luck from almost any island in the Caribbean. He may well discover a brand new highly productive fishing ground." Just to show how productive some of these waters may well be, in a recent 3 day tournament off Venezuela 312 billfish were taken. After the tournament ended the government took pains to apologize to the anglers saying they were extremely sorry that the fish were not in good supply during the days of the tournament.

Don emphasizes, that just as for most ocean fishing, season and location are of utmost importance as the fish migrate and the angler has to be at the right place at the right time to get them. Then, of course, the angler has to get one to take a hook and finally he has to fight the fish. "With the right tackle and a little luck, white marlin fishing can be a memorable experience," says the man who has taken over 200 of them.

Whenever Don Leek fished white marlin during his first two years of serious angling he always hoped he would hook into a prize blue marlin that on occasion turn up at Ocean City and Atlantic City. He didn't get any as the big fish have their own grounds. The big fish intrigued him until finally he went to

Hatteras, determined to fish until he hooked into a blue marlin. Here many anglers get their baptism of fire as this is the most productive waters for the dreadnots.

First there were several days of marvelous boatrides but no fish. Each day they took the 1½ hour trip to the edge of the Gulf Stream which is only 15 nautical miles from shore. They always knew when the boat entered the stream as the water dramatically changed color to a light tropical blue from the surrounding dark green, almost black color. Each day they set out 2 trolling lines off the outriggers and set the baits back 75 feet behind the boat. Each day the mate prepared the standard Hatteras baits of Spanish mackerel, about 18 inches long, which were gutted and sewn to the 12/0 Mustad hook. This was preceded by 15 feet of wire leader. They set an extra line flat off the back which trailed 50 feet back and finally two teasers in short completed the package which they trolled over miles and miles of ocean.

One day they trolled for several hours along a weed line, then North past the lightship and then further offshore into the stream. Don says, "It was May and the sun was hot and I was discouraged. I was getting drowsy when out of the corner of my eye I saw a big dorsal fin appear behind my bait on the line off the starboard outrigger. The line snapped off the outrigger. This was it!"

His early white marlin experience stood him well for he let the slack go out of the line and waited a second or two before throwing the reel on free spool. He carefully gloved the line going out. When he was absolutely certain that the fish had taken the bait he threw the reel in gear and lifted the rodtip pulling it back hard . . . once . . . twice . . . three times! "Got him!" He hollered. That fish exploded over the ocean tearing line from the reel. He immediately noticed the difference in the power generated by the bigger fish for the runs were longer and harder. Where the white marlin jumped and acrobated the bigger fish used brute strength and fought like a heavyweight.

Essentially Mr. Leek knew how to handle the big fish so that the difference in size did not phase him. He simply dropped the rod tip and let the fish run when it wanted line while he fanned the reel with his gloved hand so that the line would run out smoothly. When the fish stopped running he raised up the drag mechanism on his 9/0 Fin-Nor reel putting possibly 15 pounds of drag on the line and then began pumping and reeling in standard big game fashion. He really put his muscles into this one.

On a fast run the marlin broke water and started greyhounding while line raced off his reel. Mr. Leek handled it perfectly, for at this point the angler must let the fish have all the line it wants, but he must make sure the reel doesn't turn too fast and give him an overrun. If an angler makes this critical mistake a blue marlin's power will simply jerk the rod from the angler's hand and carry it overboard. Or should the angler insist on holding on after his line is snagged he may go right over the side with the rod. This has happened to a number of surprised anglers but mostly the result of such a tactical error means a popped line and a lost fish. Don held onto the reins and he worked his fish well. Within a half hour using his easy rhythm of pumping and reeling he had the fish tired and at the side for gaffing. As he brought him to the side the mate grabbed the leader while they pulled the big blue marlin to the boat.

Captain Carmey took the flying gaff when the fish was in position at the side of the boat and he stuck the hook into the soft underbelly of the fish. The handle broke off the gaff and the fish was now securely held by the heavy nylon line from the boat to the gaff handle. It was the fish's dying moments but it still thrashed in the water furiously. They dropped a tail rope around him and hoisted him over the transit and into the cockpit. Still not fully dead the fish bounced around, but a few hard smashes to its head with the club stopped it from doing any damage. When they got back to the Hatteras Marlin Club it officially weighed in at 314 pounds, and Don Leek had his first blue marlin.

Mr. Leek says that Hatteras is just the most fabulous spot on the American coast for blue marlin. He explains that the Gulf Stream which flows North along the Southern Florida coast swings out to sea at Stuart, Florida, while at the same time our shoreline bears West. In some places the two will be separated more than 100 miles, but going North beginning at South Carolina our shoreline starts swinging East again until at the Outer Banks at Hatteras the Gulf Stream will be only 15 miles from shore.

The blue marlin are in American water only a short time during certain season. Blue marlin winter in the warm Caribbean waters and only begin to move Northward in March and April depending upon the weather. The first fish will be taken off Morehead City early in April and the first ones will generally come in at Hatteras sometime before the end of the month. Then, during the month of May, fish will be raised and caught in a steady stream until finally about the first or second week in June the fishing here will reach its peak. Then fishing will begin to decline and by the time the first week of July, a blue marlin will be a rarity at Hatteras. The blue marlin will be absent here all summer but as fall progresses the marlin will again reappear in these waters. Although Hatteras fall fishing for marlin is spotty there are times in late September or October when they are caught with amazing swiftness. Then a storm may spoil it but fall fishing is just wonderful. On clear days, this angler says it is a real pleasure to get out into the warm sunshine and then break out into the clear blue water of the Gulf Stream. Mr. Leek feels like it is suddenly bursting out into another world.

The weather conditions have a great deal to do with what days the biggest of the migrations will reach the Hatteras area. At the Hatteras Marlin club they have an annual International Blue Marlin Tournament and the board of governors and tournament directors try to time the tournament so that it will coincide with the best fishing. "In 1963 we had it in the first week in June and we had a tremendous catch—97 blue marlin of which 42 were released. I even caught two in that tournament," Don says.

"The following year the tournament covered the same days, but because of a cold snap the season was late and less than 10 fish were taken by almost 50 boats fishing four days. Yet, that same year there was a tournament at Morehead City and time after time our radios crackled 'Fish on!' only to find out that it was a boat of the other tournament. That year they hit their peak season right on the head while, because of the cold we were a little premature.

"Hatteras is fortunate as the fish seem to linger here on their Northern migrations. There, of course, is the big Diamond Shoal where the shallow water has caused so many boat wrecks; but, for fishing purposes, this is a tremendous asset. The Gulf Stream comes up and sweeps right along the edges of the shoal and bait will stay here feeding along the dropoff. When the marlin come North on their migration they tend to linger in this area as it offers them an excellent feeding ground. This too helps anglers, because most fish in the area will be on feed and are ready to take a hook."

Marlin fishing is really a long extensive hunt for the fish and no matter where in the world the angler may be fishing there is never a guarantee the angler will even raise a fish, let alone catch one. He says, "I have spent a whole season where I didn't catch a single blue marlin in hundreds of hours of fishing at some of the best places in the world. There are relatively few anglers in the world that captured more than a dozen of these fish and there are less than a dozen anglers who have taken more than 100 blue marlin. I have been asked, why do we go for them? I think anyone who knows the thrill and excitement of catching a blue marlin knows why the sport is attracting new anglers in unbelievable numbers."

At the same time Don Leek does not want to be pessimistic toward any angler who can only fish on a hit an' miss chance. He tells of one day of fishing with his wife Jane (then his fiancee) and another angler. They fished less than an hour and had three marlin. Jane had hers first, a 214 pounder, his was second and it weighed in around three hundred pounds, and finally the other angler took a small one that weighed just over 100 pounds. There are other instances on record too, for the world record blue marlin was at three separate times held by anglers fishing a one shot proposition. Right at Hatteras Gary Stukes came down from New Jersey on a once a year fishing trip and chartered out with Captain William Foster, one of the local captains. Mr. Stukes took an 810 pound fish that day which held the world record for two years until a bigger one was taken in the Virgin Islands. And Mr. Leek is absolutely certain this will happen again and again. He says, "This is part of fishing."

"I feel the most important thing an angler needs to become a successful marlin angler is to have a good captain. This is just as true whether the angler charters or fishes from his own boat. It may be humbling, but it is important for an angler to remember that he can never be any better than his captain."

Captain Armond Carmey and Mr. Leek have fished together for years and he relies heavily on his captain's judgment for catching big fish. Big-game fishing is really a team effort. A good captain will know exactly where the fish are being caught. He will often be the first to spot a dorsal fin and he will know exactly how to approach a surfaced fish to get the baits in front of it without scaring it. Then during the fight he will be able to back down on the fish that may be taking too much line and he may help the angler by running with the waves instead of against them. Often he can tell when a fish is about to run or he will tell the angler of sharks gathering around a stricken fish. The angler may be in the chair all alone but the captain can help the angler by knowing when to chase a hard running fish or when he can steal a hundred yards of line by backing down on the fish. A good captain will do the 101 things that make the difference between success and failure—he is the best friend an angler has on any trip, and Mr. Leek considers captain Carney one of the best.

"Then," Don Leek said, "a mate of the caliber of Jim Baker is invaluable too. The mate prepares the baits, sees that the tackle is in order and changes the baits when they are not working right. But his most important job is handling a fish once the wire leader breaks over the side. When Jim Baker is there I don't worry because that fish will be landed. Sometimes the infighting will get real rough too and I've lost some fish on a few occasions when I was fishing without my regular crew—then you really appreciate a good mate for it is heartbreaking for any angler to lose a fish that is ready for boating."

Blue marlin anglers have a wide choice of tackle. Generally, Don suggests, that a beginner start with 130 pound class outfits including a 130 pound class rod, a 12/0 reel and 130 pound test dacron line. He says, "This outfit gives the angler margin for error. The angler may well be able to get away with a certain amount of slack line that could at times develop during a fight and on hard runs he could put more drag on the line thus tiring the fish faster. However, the experienced angler would in all probability enjoy the added thrills of fishing with somewhat lighter tackle. I think an 80 pound class outfit probably best suits Atlantic blue marlin fishing. I do much of my fishing with a glass rod, 80 pound class, a 9/0 Fin-Nor Reel and dacron line of 80 pound test. With this tackle I can handle any blue marlin in the Atlantic Ocean."

Don also explains he has taken blue marlin on 50 pound class tackle, but he would not suggest tackle this light until an angler has captured at least a half a dozen fish. With tackle of this test, whenever the marlin is large than 300 pounds, it takes real skill of the angler and the captain to take the fish. One mistake and the line pops faster than a balloon in a New Year's Eve party. The angler cannot allow any slack at any time and he cannot raise the drag, consequently he must pump the rod and reel precisely right so as to get that fishes mouth open and tire and drown him.

To illustrate Mr. Leek's skill there was one marlin he took on 50 pound test line while fishing in a tournament. This tournament gives ½ point extra per pound for fish taken on 50 pound test tackle thus enticing angler to lighten the tackle. He hooked the fish and then by applying just the right amount of pressure at the right time the fish was worn out in ten minutes of fighting and was boated in 13 minutes. That fish weighed 311 pounds.

There was another fish at Bimini which was the biggest Mr. Leek had ever hooked. "I was using a 50 pound class outfit and it was a huge one. That fish swallowed the bait and took off all over the ocean—what dynamic fury. But gradually I managed to work him in close to the boat and got my first look—it was huge, like a gigantic bull with eyes as big as baseballs. This one went way over 500 pounds—way over. He took off and I worked extremely careful. I let line out and then bent into my rod when I could open his mouth and work him. Several times I wished I had heavier tackle but I was getting the job done. Within an hour and a half I had the fish all the way to the side of the boat and the leader broke over the side. My regular mate wasn't with me as I was fishing on a strange boat. I saw the way he handled a gaff—this mate was fish shy. Gaffing a big fish can be extremely dangerous because that monster had tremendous strength and if the gaff is not in the organs of the fish it simply becomes a club the fish can use to destroy the hull of the boat. It was too obvious the mate was shy and didn't know what he was doing so I shouted for him to let go of the leader and I let the fish out again with the thoughts of working him further. I worked him another half hour and had him in close again, but still that marlin was too green for a novice to handle so I tried a third time. I knew I would have to bring that fish in 95% dead to capture it. Finally after 2 hours and 35 minutes of fighting I realized that under the circumstances I had lost, for with the light tackle I really couldn't get the fish so tired he would come in practically belly up. There were sharks starting to come around by then so I simply ordered the line cut. It was heartbreaking as this blue marlin certainly would have beaten the existing 50 pound class International Game Fish Association world record of 551 pounds. I knew if I had Jim Baker there once that leader broke over the side that fish would have been mine."

This expert says there are several ways to handle a hooked fish. In a tournament the angler may want the fish in a hurry so when he gets in the chair he straps on the shoulder holster or kidney holster, then he keeps the drag up high and really works the fish. The object is to open the fishes mouth and force water down his throat to drown the fish. The angler keeps full pressure on the fish at all times and the fish is never given a chance to act up. When fighting the angler pulls the rod tip up in a smooth easy rhythm and then drops the rod tip and while doing so reels in the line he has gained. Immediately he again pulls the rod back, repeating the motion over and over again. Only when a fish runs does the angler stop the motion and give the fish line, but the moment it ceases running, it's back to work. With relentless pressure of this type, Mr. Leek feels an angler using 130 pound test tackle should have a 300 pound blue marlin ready for boating within 15 minutes.

As the tackle is lightened it extends the length of the battle because the drag must be lowered and pressure cannot be so forcefully applied. A 300 pound fish hooked by an angler using 80 pound test tackle should take 20 to 30 minutes. With 50 pound class outfits it is more of the same, however, requiring more finesse and reliance on the captain's ability to follow a fish when possible. Most of the fight is still the anglers and with skill he should boat a 300 pound fish in 30 to 45 minutes.

Anglers often gamble using light tackle in a tournament as special points are awarded to the angler for using lighter tackle. As an example, at some tournaments points are awarded for fish caught in the following manner: 130 pound class tackle—1 point per pound or 300 points for a released fish; 80 pound class tackle —1¼ point per pound or 375 points for a released fish; 50 pound class tackle—1½ point per pound or 450 points for a released fish.

In a tournament an angler must land his fish in two hours or he gets no points and he must capture the fish without broken rods and without the fish being sharked or mutilated. He says, "I was in several tournaments where anglers using light tackle lost tournaments only because they broke their rods. Whenever an angler goes to 50 pound class tackle for blue marlin it is a gamble but a temptingly good one.

"I have a chronic bad back and on occasion it really gives me trouble and I have to watch myself for a while. I have fished a number of times with my back acting up and at those times I learned more about taking a fish than ever before. I had to take my fish without strength as I simply did not have any. I learned that anyone can handle a marlin, and that goes from a 100 pound girl on up. The whole secret is in the drag—lower the drag to 5 to 7 pounds of pressure and it simply does not take much strength to pull the rod back. A high drag line won't give off the reel and the angler pulls on the fish. However, with a low drag line easily gives off the reel as the angler pulls on the rod and little strength is required. When my back is bad I use a holster, drop the drag way down and do the fighting using only my arms and not straining my back."

He laughs and explains that some high spirited fish will really take them for a Nantucket sleigh ride, but with patience and a good crew they were taken. Mr. Leek once took a 242 pound marlin when his back was so bad he could hardly stand up. But he explains, "I love fishing and just had to give it a try. It was an education too, for I really learned how to handle a fish as I made every move count." It could possibly be explained the same way it is with baseball pitchers who admit they didn't learn how to pitch until they had a sore arm and couldn't rely simply on speed and strength.

Other spots American anglers regularly fish blue marlin include the ports out of Southern Florida anywhere from West Palm Beach to Miami and out of the Keys. Most of the time the blue marlin are found in the Gulf Stream and the fishing seems best further out in the stream near one of the Bahama Islands. This generally makes for a lengthy boatride, but this tropical water is gorgeous and a day out is a pleasure for any angler.

The Bahama Islands are of course famous for their blue marlin fishing. Some of the best blue marlin fishing in the world is done off Bimini, Walker Cay and Chub Cay. Fishing at these hotspots starts about February every year and is excellent right through July. April and May are probably peak months and at such places as Bimini there will be a good supply of blue marlin taken right through the end of July. Andros Island offers blue marlin fishing through the winter months. The 50 pound test line record fish was taken at Andros Island in February 1960.

If anyone wants to see just how good Bahama marlin fishing is he has only to look into the official International Game Fish Association Book of World Record Marine Fish. Bimini, is all over the record book both for men and women's records on the various test lines. These islands have had record catches taken during the months of April, June and July indicating clearly the tremendous fishing available during spring and early summer.

There are several things Mr. Leek likes about marlin fishing in the Bahamas. One is that the fish seem to fight with more fury than those taken further North. He feels the reason for this is that a marlin is basically a tropical fish and has a metabolism best suited for tropical waters. As the fish migrate North the water temperature may fall only a few degrees but it seems to make a difference in its actions. He says, "I have had fish on the hook while fishing Bimini that fight furiously while those I caught further North just don't react quite as violently. This has been my experience both with blue as well as white marlin, and other anglers I have talked with confirm this belief."

Another item of the island fishing that is appealing is that the angler can begin fishing just a few minutes out of port. The nice thing about this is that in a typical ten hour fishing day the lines will be in the water for 9½ hours as opposed to having the baits out only 6 hours in the same 10 hour fishing day from another location.

The first choice of baits at Bimini is mullet. These are flown in daily from Florida and have become pretty much the standard bait throughout the Bahamas. The mullet is, of course, always a good bait because rigged on a 12/0 hook it swims well in the water. Marlin go for them because they are used to feeding on this type and size fish. They are always an excellent bait as they are quite resilient in the water and hold together well. However, an angler can get the big marlin to hit Spanish mackerel, ballyhoo, bonita or any other fish in the 12 to 20 inch size for actually it has been proved marlin are not fussy feeders. Squid, when the angler can get them the right size, will work fine too. Also, they can be caught on artificial baits such as the Hawaiian Knucklehead. "I don't like these because I feel the real baits offer more challenge."

Reviewing the blue marlin fishing of the Atlantic and Caribbean Don Leek mentions one other fine spot extensively fished by Americans and that is Puerto Rico. When talking about Puerto Rican fishing he breaks into a broad grin and says, "Puerto Rico offers fine marlin fishing, but I don't think there are quite as many fish there as the natives would like to have you believe. I remember one tournament and every two minutes the radio blared 'blue marlin on—oh we lost it.' This went on for four days and when everything was finished I think there were only a dozen marlin taken during the four days. In that tournament everything that hit the line—dolphin, bonita, sharks was a blue marlin. Some of the boys were seeing phantom marlin." Don takes great pleasure out of teasing the Puerto Rican anglers since there is quite a friendly rivalry going between Hatteras anglers and Puerto Rican marlin anglers as each group feels theirs is absolutely the best spot in the world for the fish.

Mr. Leek then gets back to serious angling advice and says that Puerto Rico has blue marlin off its shores all year long but from past angling records the best fishing is during the summer months extending well into the fall. Fishing here begins to get productive about the middle of June and is excellent in July, August and September and into October. After that the catches will taper off in number.

The Virgin Islands are the current proud holder of the world record fish, taken there by John Battles and weighing in at 814 pounds. This fish was taken on 80 pound class tackle by an experienced angler and now is the 80 pound and all tackle world record. The season for blue marlin at the Virgin Islands is basically the same season as that of Puerto Rico—summer and fall for blue marlin.

There are opportunities to hook blue marlin in just about

every square mile of tropical water. Generally, the best spots are near steep dropoffs. Baitfish congregate there to feed, thus bringing in the marlin to feed off them. Take any Caribbean Island and chances are that if it were fished in big-game style it would produce marlin. Jamaica is now coming into its own. Then the Northern coast of South America offers some excellent opportunities at known spots off Venezuela and Aruba. There are fish off Brazil as well as off Africa. There are countless unknown grounds throughout this vast area and any angler with adventure in his soul could look for new fishing grounds, which, when found always create excitement.

Mr. Leek then talked about the excellent billfishing of the West Coast, but first he went on to say that in no manner should he be considered an expert on West Coast billfishing, "I just haven't done enough fishing in the Pacific to really know all the intricacies."

However, several years ago he did make a movie called, "Tigers of the Sea" at La Paz, Mexico. Here he hooked into several striped marlin and sailfish and had real fun making the film. "I really learned to appreciate the fine fishing offered in Mexico because all the anglers in the film had good action and took fish. I know there were several instances where some pretty good anglers went to make movies and with all the expensive equipment around the fish wouldn't cooperate, but in La Paz the fishing was so good we had no trouble." The film is available free for showing at clubs by writing to Pacemaker at Egg Harbor, New Jersey.

He has also fished the other fine spots of Mexico including Mazatlan, Acapulco and Guaymas, but he prefers not to expound on this fishing as he simply does not think he has fished enough here to criticize.

Generally, Mr. Leek compares the western striped marlin to the eastern white marlin in both size and spirit. Both fish are the smallest of the marlin family in their particular ocean and the most common, however, the striped marlin will average 50 pounds more in weight than the white. Both are taken from the top sportsfishing ports and both are tremendously exciting fish to hook, taking off, jumping, tailwalking and raising great fury.

He points out some of the different methods of fishing used by Mexican anglers for they seldom put a bait in the water until a fish is spotted. This is done partly as the anglers want to concentrate on billfish and not get the sharks that are also plentiful. "The water is very clear here, but I have had so many marlin just come up from the deep behind my bait that it seems only logical to me that if they splashed their baits around they would catch themselves some extra fish."

The other big fish of the Pacific is, of course, the Pacific blue marlin. Some ichtiologists consider it a different specie from the Atlantic blue marlin while others insist it is exactly the same fish. One thing is certain that the captures of the Pacific marlin show clearly that the fish attains a greater weight in the Pacific as any number of fish have been taken that weighed over 1,000 pounds while our Atlantic best is just over 800 pounds. In Mexico they are generally baited when sighted with the dorsal fins protruding while at Hawaii they will be fished by using artificial baits trolled around. The artificials are the predominate baits at Hawaii as the best of them such as the Hawaiian Knucklehead and other types of knuckleheads were invented and developed by island anglers.

Another Pacific spot that is really drawing American anglers is Panama, where the Club de Pesca has become a winter meeting ground for the regular marlin adherents. It is tremendous fishing too, with Pacific sailfish, striped marlin, blue marlin and even black marlin the regular captures. The fishing styles used by the captains are similar to the Mexican styles and the results are spectacular with triples not at all unusual.

Mr. Leek has never caught any of the most incredible fish of the ocean—the black marlin. This Pacific ocean marlin is the biggest of all gamefish with the current world record set at 1,560 pounds. They are found in widely scattered areas of the Pacific with some taken off Hawaii, in the Gulf of Panama, but the biggest ones and the largest concentrations are found off

South America in the Humbolt current. One of the real hot spots for this fish is the small town of Cabo Blanco in Peru.

Although a fish of 1560 pounds seems truly incredible Mr. Leek has talked with some anglers who regularly fish Cabo Blanco and they confirm this is not an exceedingly large fish for this area. One angler tells of seeing a 2,200 pound specimen lying on the beach. This fish had been harpooned commercially as marlin meat is an important food item here.

Tackle for these fish is geared to big fish and is 130 pound test with 12/0 reels. Terminal tackle is either wire or cable with big 12/0 hooks, while the baits that are used would be prize catches for many stateside anglers. The favorite one is a bonito about 2 or 3 feet long while dolphins or tuna of the same size are also used. There have been black marlin found with fish over 100 pounds in their stomach so that baits must be kept large to entice a monster.

Cabo Blanco is a fascinating place and although it is only a few degrees South of the equator it is cold at sea because of the Humboldt Current that passes only a few miles offshore. This cold current sweeps North up the West coast of South America and brings the abundance of forage fish which in turn attract the large fish. It is right at Cabo Blanco that the current begins a Western turn, and here the best of the concentrations of the really huge black marlin are found.

The water in the Humboldt current is rough and cold and when anglers go out they start a hunt for dorsal fins. The fish will not be baited until sighted, at which time the prepared bait is dropped over the side and the captain makes an approach for the fish. If one strikes it is a memorable fishing trip as fights generally extend from 2 to 4 hours. Anglers that have taken a black marlin say it is just an incredible experience as there is nothing equal to it in fishing.

With air transportation as good as it is today anglers can get to these out-of-the-way spots much easier than ever before, and men like Mr. Leek regularly pore over their busy schedules to see just when they can squeeze in a fishing trip to some exotic place.

This marvelous angler says, "There are so many things I want to do in fishing." Among them is he wants to get a really big blue marlin and another thing is he wants a black marlin. If you want to bet on a man to beat some existing world marlin record you couldn't go far off by betting on Mr. Donald Leek—many anglers do.

9. SWORDFISHING WITH ED GRUBER

Prior to 1950 when an angler took one swordfish in his life it was considered the ultimate moment of a highly successful fishing career, for until the middle 1950's it was estimated that less than 500 swordfish had ever been taken by rod and reel anglers all over the world. Since then a new group of deep-sea anglers have dramatically improved this score. By intensively fishing and introducing totally new methods, they have revolutionized this most demanding and exciting fishing.

Mr. Ed Gruber, President of Spring City Knitting Company in Pennsylvania, is one of the foremost swordfishermen in the country. He alone has taken 28 swordfish over a 6 year span and in one year 1958, he took a fantastic total of 11 fish. On five different occasions he has taken 2 fish in a single day for when the fish are there he relentlessly hunts them. Mr. Gruber has developed his own methods of swordfishing which cannot be found in any book. He has, by experimenting and through the process of trial and error, extended his skill to taking these fish to a point where his results are comparable to the results other anglers obtain going for other big game specie which are somewhat simpler to capture.

Swordfishing for Mr. Gruber begins in late June when the

fish arrive at the best U.S. swordfishing ground, the famous triangle stretching from Shinnecock Long Island to No Man's Land to Nantucket. During the first weeks of the season the fish will be sighted in the Shinnecock area and they sometimes are spotted only a few miles from shore. Gradually as the summer progresses the main concentration of fish shifts further offshore and by late August the biggest number of swordfish will be in the area of Martha's Vineyard and Nantucket. The fish will stay there in number until the first big storm in September which means the end of swordfishing. The disrupted and colder water drives the fish down and no more swordfish will be sighted until the following year.

This new breed of swordfishermen take their sport extremely serious and work exceedingly hard at it. For Ed Gruber a day of swordfishing means flying to Montauk Point in the evening so that he can be at his boat at the Deep Sea Club before dawn the next morning. Once aboard his 44 foot Rybovich Sportsfisherman which he lovingly calls the *Nitso,* named after his business of knitting and sewing, he may check over some charts with Captain William Holzman to plan the day's hunt. The captain will already have the baits in the cooler all prepared with hooks inserted and ready for fishing. The rod will be in the rodholder in the cockpit where it will remain until a fish is actually sighted. If fishing is bad and no fish are sighted weeks could go by without the line on the reel ever getting wet; however, on other days this same line may be required to hold a 600 pound fighting mad swordfish for 3 to 5 hours of intensive fighting. Just before he leaves port Mr. Gruber automatically checks his rod, reel and line.

Then the captain starts the motors and they head for open water where the first phase of the action begins—the Hunt! Fisherman Ed Gruber, Captain Bill Holzman and the mate take their position on the tower of the boat 20 feet above the water where they can best scan the ocean. The *Nitso* will proceed through the water mile after mile and all the while the men will be watching the ocean surface for those dorsal fins that could spell swordfish. To aid their search they will snap on the radio and listen in on various fishermen that are talking. Some of the best leads they have had came from commercial fishermen that have spotted a dorsal fin in their area. When this occurs it's a big rush into the cabin to study the charts in an effort to locate the area. If they can localize the report they quickly head in that direction. Sometimes these reports are not reliable and often a fish will have sounded by the time they get there or worse another commercial fisherman may have harpooned the fish. Still, surfaced swordfish are rare and any and every report of one warrants a run for the area.

Each day's hunt will cover miles of ocean. A typical trip would begin at Montauk with a quick run for the Shinnecock Inlet area. From there it is offshore going out approximately 90 miles to the spot referred to as the Banana at Nantucket. This is usually the furthest point of their trip before they begin the 90 mile hunt back. As they make this run they travel along the 150 or 180 foot line for these are the ledges where the swordfish feed.

The search for the fish is so hard and so extensive that many of the anglers consider it a successful day if they merely sight a fish. To give some idea of the extent of these hunts, in one year Mr. Gruber covered over 7,000 miles of water during 41 full days of fishing where he sighted 28 swordfish. Others years it was much the same story except one fantastic year, 1958 where he spotted 50 swordfish in just 21 days of fishing sighting an average of more than 2 a day. The sight of a dorsal fin gives these men the same elation a hunter feels who after miles of tracking finally gets a clear view of his quarry.

Mr. Gruber says, "We stand on the tower and we search every mile of ocean for the fish. We have developed a kind of competition between the three of us to see who can spot one. Sighting the fish is always a problem but it is worst when the water is rough, for then it is almost impossible to see a fin. Some days it's easy to see them and a perfect day is when the ocean is as smooth as a big lake for then those dorsal fins really stick up. Another time I have had exceedingly good luck in sighting swordfish is in a fog. A dense heavy fog will make the water just as calm as could be and it seems to help bring the fish up and on several occasions we have practically run one down. They seem less shy then and once we came within 30 yards of one. To get this one we merely ran down off the tower and threw the bait out and he took it."

Sighting some of the fish is difficult because they will be up near the surface but will be completely submerged. These fish will be just lazily swimming along just under the surface of the water, and Captain Bill Holzman seems most adapt at sighting these. Other times just a small section of a fin will show above the water and these too must be spotted and fished. Mr. Gruber prides himself at being able to find these fish. The sight they all dream about is a big one sitting up on the surface as high as a duck in a shooting gallery.

Not all sighted dorsal fins turn out to be swordfish for occasionally sharks will temporarily fool them. Usually a swordfish will have the dorsal and tail fins above water and upon examination it can be distinguished from sharks because its tail fin is rigid while the tail fins of a shark will flop from side to side. When an investigation of a fish turns out to be a shark they quickly move away because the chances are that there will be no swordfish in the immediate area. However, should the sighted dorsal fin prove to be a swordfish then phase one—the hunt—of this difficult and demanding sport is finished.

Phase two—the stalking—demands that the angler get the fish to take a bait. This can be frustrating for swordfish that are on the surface are full and are on top only to rest. Thus the angler has the problem of persuading a fish that is full to take his bait. Just how difficult this is quickly shows up in Mr. Gruber's statistics for he feels if he can induce 30% of the fish he sights to strike he is doing exceedingly well. His own records are impressive yet they vary from his worst year when he spotted 64 fish and had only 15 strikes, to a more typical year when he managed 16 strikes from 43 sighted fish thus averaging approximately 40%. During his best year of fishing in 1958 he had an incredible 25 strikes from the 50 fish he sighted. If this were baseball you would say he batted 500 that year, but baseball or fishing, this average was outstanding.

Much experimentation has been done by Mr. Gruber on the best way to present a bait to a swordfish. Several years back he would have huge California squid delivered to him for the idea was that no fish—no matter how full—could resist a meal like that. These were big squid and they worked fine but still there were always those frustrating times when the fish just wouldn't take. Angler Ed Gruber admits that possibly no bait will ever turn out to be the perfect bait simply because the angler is trying to present food to a fish that is not feeding. Thus after the California squid, he began experimenting with other baits including ballyhoo, mackerel, mullet and others but he had no luck with any of these. However, he always went back to squid but this time instead of using the huge squid he came down to smaller ones and tried those only a foot or so in length. The captain was able to insert smaller hooks, using 10/0's, in this bait and generally it made a bait that was more deceptive. Mr. Gruber also reasoned that because these fish are full, they will not be looking for a large meal, yet the delicious small meal presented in a tantalizing method directly in front of a fish will be irresistable. This is very similar to a person who has just eaten a meal who would never touch another meal, yet he might be induced to nibble on mints.

Once the dorsal fin is sighted, all hands aboard the *Nitso* know their job. Angler Ed Gruber climbs down off the tower and takes his place in the fighting chair. He takes his rod out of the holder and places it in the gimbal. Quickly he checks the drag for he wants to make sure it is set at about 18 to 20 pounds. Now he throws his reel on free spool because on the approach to the fish, a considerable quantity of line must be let out quickly. The mate, who will be standing next to Mr. Gruber, snaps on the squid bait to the leader and they begin their first cautious approach to the fish.

At this point the Captain is the most important member of the team for he must maneuver the boat so that the bait comes right in front of the fish while neither the wake from the boat, or the bait spook the resting fish. Often the swordfish will be moving slowly thus the captain must time his maneuver so that the angler's bait which is at the end of 250 to 300 feet of line will come within 30 feet of the fishes bill. Generally, fine captains like Bill Holzman try to approach a fish by keeping the sun to the angler's back for they know that vision plays an important part of proper timing of the strike. If the angler has the sun in his eyes he can completely lose sight of his fish and this could lead to ill timed strikes and lost fish.

The captain's problem is made more difficult by the fact that he can only approach a fish at 4 to 6 knots for the bait must slide through the water as quietly as a live squid. A skipping bait can scare a fish and will look unnatural. Once the captain maneuvers the trailing bait so that it gets within 30 feet of the fish's bill he slows the boat so that the bait gets a chance to settle down in front of the fish. They always keep the bait moving slightly, for they have had no luck with an absolutely still bait. The swordfish will see the bait and he may go for it or he may simply sit there completely oblivious of the offering in front of him. If this happens the captain moves the boat away, circles, and comes in for another approach to the fish.

During the tense approach the angler and mate are busy too. The reel will be on free spool and the angler will let out between 250 to 300 feet of line. As the line goes out Mr. Gruber fans the reel with his (left) gloved hand to prevent overruns or backlashes. His glove is a simple cotton glove which he wets with seawater. This, incidently, is one of the most important pieces of his equipment for in his unique method of battling swordfish he repeatedly uses the glove to augment the drag on the reel.

As the bait reaches the critical point in front of the fish they wait to see if the fish takes the bait. If the fish moves for it the mate will begin stripping off 50 to 100 feet of line from the angler's reel and laying it in the water. On some fast hits there is no time for this maneuver and the angler merely sets the hook, but for most swordfish hits, the extra dead line is important as there must be absolutely no interference with the fish taking the bait.

Of course when the fish nudges the bait and spits it out it means reeling in, circling and going through the whole process, again trying to be just a little more careful the next time. The second pass will be a repeat of the first one, and if the fish again refuses the bait, it will have to be lines in and one more try. During past times, the anglers used to give up when a fish wouldn't strike, but the modern angler has learned to keep trying until the fish either takes the bait or sounds.

Ed Gruber recalls one fish he took was hooked on the 12th pass. He says, "By this time we were so angry we didn't care if the fish took it or not and on that final approach our bait was actually skipping on the water as it passed him. He just upped and really smashed at it that time. I certainly was surprised and do not recommend this type of approach, for the slow easy one works best; but, when everything else failed, it worked that time for us."

Swordfish have good eyes and they will see any bait that is put in front of them. If they are in a taking mood they will move toward the bait, coming at it from the back or the side. Mr. Gruber states, "Almost 70% of all swordfish are foul hooked because when that fish comes at the bait, he can really bang the wire leader and many times will twist it all around himself. A foul hooked fish often starts his battle with water splashing in all directions. Other times when they hit the bait, a hook may slide into one of their fins and this usually means a lightly hooked fish that is dangerous to handle. If the fish gets the line wrapped around his tail it completely ruins the fight. The fishes most powerful muscles are in his tail for he uses these to propel himself, thus if his tail is of no use to him he consequently has no ability to fight. No sportsman wants to catch a fish like that—there isn't any fight to them."

The fish that hit the softest are the ones where the hook is in or near the mouth. When the fish does get the bait he will take it and begin to run with it. Angler Ed Gruber will have his reel on free spool but the drag is preset at about 20 pounds, so that when the reel is snapped into gear there will be plenty of pressure. At this critical point when the fish takes the bait and begins to run, Mr. Gruber will watch the slack line that is in the water. He will permit the fish to take all of this line plus some additional line from the reel, but suddenly when he feels it is time he snaps the reel in gear and he starts winding until the line comes tight or he feels the fish. Then he strikes the fish hard! This expert swordfisherman says, "I strike the line as hard as I can—5, 6, 7 or even 8 times. If I am going to lose the fish I want to lose him right now, because I will be fighting that fish anywhere up to 4 hours and I don't want him to break off at the end of that time."

A perfectly set hook will sink deep into the bone in a swordfish's mouth and that fish will be on to stay. However, since most hooks never get into the bone and only pierce the fleshy parts of the fish's mouth it is essential that the angler handle each fish with extreme care not to rip the hook from the fish.

Now phase three—the battle—begins and Ed Gruber warns that the angler should be ready for the newly hooked fish to streak off on a gigantic run. This angler's reel is in gear on the strike but as soon as the fish begins running he drops the drag while dipping his rod tip down. He reduces the drag to a point where there will only be two or three pounds of pressure left while with fingers extended he places his left gloved hand down on the spool of the reel and presses to add pressure. Then throughout the fight he will add or release pressure as the situation warrants. Thus this angler in effect has supplemented the reel drag with the gloved hand. This method gives the fisherman delicate control of how much pressure he can safely put on a fish at any given second. Mr. Gruber has shifted the emphasis for fighting a big swordfish from muscle to deft and timing. Against a swordfish too much strain means a pulled hook, and Mr. Gruber's method has saved him many fish and upped his percentage of captures considerably.

He learned early that deft is what takes swordfish. He says, "My first summer of swordfishing followed a bad spring of marlin fishing where I had broken a number of fish off. When I had my first swordfish on the captain said, 'Let's give him the kid glove treatment.' I answered that we will give him a satin glove treatment and as a result I immediately began experimenting with the least amount of drag I could put on a line and it proved to be the answer."

Although all the fish are different many of them will begin a fight with a long hard run. Immediately at its conclusion this angler starts bringing the fish in, but he does not pump and reel in standard big-game fashion. Mr. Gruber says, "I have my drag set so low that it is only powerful enough to take up line on the spool as I crank the reel. I begin by cranking hard to get the slack or the big bow that may have developed during the run out of the line. I naturally want to bring the fish into the boat as close as possible for we try to do most of the fighting within 50 yards of the boat. If he starts to run while I am bringing him in I just let him go and I go back to pressing on the spool with my gloved hand. I have fought some fish so long that when I was through my left hand was so stiff from pressing against the reel that I could hardly move it."

Mr. Gruber explains that an angler never really knows just what a fish will do during a fight. He says that most of them will take at least 2 long hard runs while some of them will come up, tail walk on the water and just shake their heads furiously. Some will greyhound and he has had them take as many as 15 jumps during a fight. When a fish jumps, Mr. Gruber will lift his rod up in an effort to lift as much line as possible out of the water as the line in the water can give a fish enough drag to pull a hook loose.

"Some of them really get furious," he explains. "I have had one charge our boat and go straight for our stern. The fish charged and took a furious leap but the captain was watching and he sped the boat away. Still that fish only missed our stern by less than a yard. Another one suddenly started greyhounding and he leaped over at least ¼ of our cockpit splashing back in the water on the starboard side. One of the boats at Montauk was hit by a charging swordfish and its sword went right into the planking and broke. You know, they couldn't get that piece of sword out of the hull until the winter when the boat was lifted out of the water."

Other fish will sound and will doggedly want to battle it out below the surface. When this happens Mr. Gruber will increase his drag to 12 or more pounds of pressure in an effort to force the fish to come up. This increase in pressure is dangerous but when a fish is down it is the only thing an angler can do because he has to get him out of deep water or he will surely lose the fish.

Angler Ed Gruber explains, "I try to work my fish in close to the boat by carefully bringing him in and letting him go when he wants to. These battles with swordfish could go on 3, 4 or more hours, but when I feel that the fish is tiring, I gradually increase the drag to put more pressure on him. This helps tire him faster and finally get him to the side of the boat.

"After an hour or two of fighting I may get the fish to the boat and at this time we estimate just what shape he is in. If the fish is not exhausted, I let him run out again because landing a swordfish is an extremely difficult thing. When we feel he is ready, the mate will grab the wire leader as it comes over the side and he will hand line the leader in. I throw the reel on free spool because if the fish wants to run, the angler must give him all the line he wants for in these close quarters any slight mistake means a lost fish. Our final test to see if the fish is ready for landing is as the mate pulls in the leader. On my boat the mate never twists his hand around the leader nor does he wind the wire around anything. If the mate can pull the leader in, the fish is ready for gaffing and if the mate cannot pull the leader to him and the fish puts up a strong resistance we know he is not ready. Then he goes out for another fight. It is simply too dangerous to try to land a green swordfish for not only are the chances of losing him great but even if he is landed he can really smash things up on board."

Point four—the landing—begins now and Mr. Gruber goes on to say, "When the mate easily brings the leader in we quickly put a flying gaff into the fish. We try to place it under or near the dorsal fin. As soon as the gaff is in him we break the line off the flying gaff and tie it to the boat. Now we put a second gaff into the fish trying to place it near the tail. This will help hold him as we drop the tailrope on him. Once you get a tailrope on a fish and tighten it he is your fish. After that we simply haul him through the transom and into the cockpit. Once in the boat if he acts up the mate will hit him over the head with a club to quiet him because 400 pounds of angry swordfish can be dangerous. Some of these fish put up their hardest fight when they get in the boat. It's funny with swordfish, for you may find some that are lethargic in the water then right at the end go wild while others will be absolutely wild in the ocean and then come in like gentlemen. I once had a fish on for over two hours and I just couldn't seem to tire him and then I saw him jump—he was one of the smallest fish I ever took, hardly weighing 150 pounds, but what a scrapper. You just never know with them."

To illustrate the pitch of excitement this fishing can reach Mr. Gruber tells of one of the fish he landed. "I was bringing him in when three sharks began circling the fish. He looked completely ready for landing so I brought him up to the boat and we quickly sunk the flying gaff into him. Instantly, this fish seemed to spring to life for he dove right under the boat. He went down so hard and fast that he ripped the gaff through his body and it slipped out. Then he churned and took off while he twisted my line around the rudder post of the boat. I thought this was surely a lost fish, but luckily this one had the hook deep in the bone of his mouth. The hook was still in him as he swam back and forth. We all knew that if we wanted that fish the line would have to be freed from the rudder post and with three sharks circling the injured fish it would only be a matter of time before they attacked. I was giving thoughts to cutting him off so that he could escape the sharks.

"Captain Bill Holzman acted fast and he quickly got a line and tied one of the squid from the cooler on it. He dropped the rig over the side to the sharks and one grabbed it. The captain pulled the shark in and lifted its head over the side of the boat. He grabbed a club and smashed the shark on the head killing it. Then he baited up again and took the second shark and finally he killed the third one.

"We were all tense with the excitement and without a word from anyone the mate jumped overboard and untangled my line from the rudder post. The captain ran to the controls to get the boat in position for me to fight and I had to yell because in the tense moments we almost forgot the mate in the water. He quickly climbed aboard and I resumed the battle.

"The fish had been weakened by the gash in him and before long we boated him. We were amazed to see that the gaff had ripped 2 feet through his body. It showed us how strong these swordfish really are. I was extremely lucky that this was a perfectly hooked fish for otherwise I wouldn't have had a chance to get him."

The moment a fight is concluded aboard the *Nitso* it is back to the tower and immediately resume the hunt for another fish. If one fish was taken it means they are up that day and that is how on June 28 and July 26, 1958, July 11, 1959, September 9, 1961 and September 9, 1963 angler Ed Gruber took doubles. This angler's ambition is for a triple and in U.S. waters that has only been done by one man. Mr. Gruber would very much like to equal that mark.

One point Mr. Gruber makes is to properly fish, the angler needs good equipment. For swordfish he uses an 80 pound test tip Tycoon Rod combined with a 9/0 Fin-Nor reel. He has done much experimenting with the lines he uses. Originally he used only 24 thread linen lines but then he swung over to the braided dacron and he also tried monofilament. Each of these synthetics had certain advantages but they also had disadvantages. Then he hit upon a revolutionary idea that utilized the best qualities of each of these. The monofilament had stretch which made it hard to break and it could take sudden hard shocks, but because of the stretch, it acted badly on a reel and had a tendency to choke a reel. The braided dacron on the other hand lacked stretch and could be snapped more easily by sudden unexpected shock, but it acted admirably on a reel. Mr. Gruber solved his problem when he wound 500 yards of 80 pound test braided dacron on his reel and then added 200 feet of 80 pound test monofilament between the dacron and the leader. This short section of monofilament absorbed much of the shock of the fighting fish and saved broken lines. The two lines are connected by a small clamp that has a little swivel in it. To make this connection so that it doesn't injure or foul the guides on the rod this angler painstakenly wraps dental floss over the connection. This makes the connecting link appear only as a small bump on the line. Mr. Gruber feels this combination line has saved him several breakoffs and in this way he gets the best from both lines.

The leader too has been subjected to this anglers scrutiny. He first fished using cable with the thought it would hold best and would be less likely to kink or break from repeated smashes of the fish's sword. He took fish with cable for it did the job admirably but still he felt that it was too visible in the water and he was sure in some cases it spooked some fish. He began experimenting with wire which he found far more deceptive, but of course he is well aware that it increased the danger of breakoff. Still, he feels the added danger is well worth the gamble for unless the angler can induce a swordfish to hit he won't catch him anyway.

Hooks for this fishing have also been changed where his original hooks were big 12/0 Sobey that he placed in the giant California squid. He has cut down on the size of the baits using regular squid about a foot long into which he inserts two 10/0 Sobey hooks that are laid so that they lie flat and are completely hidden. The International Game Fish Association permits 2 hook setups as long as they are at least a hook's length apart and not more than 18 inches apart. His rig completely complies with this requirement for he would have it no other way. The combination of a smaller bait and smaller hooks add deception which is of the utmost importance to get a swordfish to strike.

There is currently concern among sportsmen regarding the extent of the commercial swordfishing off Long Island and Southern New England. The commercial harpooners are now employing airplanes as spotters to lead them to surfaced fish and in that way they take many hundreds of fish yearly. They are also employing long lining methods for swordfish and one boat out of Wood's Hole, Massachusetts, came back with a catch of 300 swordfish. This boat used the Japanese Long Line method which baited hooks every few feet. These captures of course showed anglers that there are many more swordfish in the area than ever thought to be, but just how many there are no one knows. If this relentless pressure continues the anglers are gravely concerned that it could destroy the supply of fish, thus ruining fishing for the sportsmen as well as the commercial anglers.

What does Mr. Gruber think of the future of swordfishing in America? He says, "It is growing all the time for more and more anglers are learning to fish these superb sportsfish. Every year I see more boat owners adding towers to their crafts and that is done for only one reason—to hunt swordfish."

This marvelous angler who has caught swordfish weighing as much as 575 pounds, has fought battles that lasted four hours and more, has also tasted the frustration of the sport for in one whole season he once took only one fish. Other years he took 11, 6 and 5 respectively, and continually ranked with the best. Mr. Gruber knows this fishing like no other angler, for to him the swordfish hunt—the stalking—the fight and the excitement of landing one of these fish add up to the finest sport in the world. It is no wonder Mr. Gruber says, "I would rather go out and catch no swordfish than to take three fish of another kind." As for him, nothing else compares.

10. GIANT BLUEFIN TUNA FISHING WITH HARRY PETERS

Shortly after "Giant Bluefin Tuna Fishing with Harry Peters" was written Mr. Harry Peters died suddenly. The entire sports fishing world was shocked and I felt a personal loss as Mr. Peters was the first angler I interviewed for this book. He encouraged me to go on with this unusual idea for a fishing book and went so far as to arrange an introduction to several other top deep-sea anglers for me.

I left the article entirely intact and it appears exactly the way he approved of it. I hope it can stand as kind of a memory of this sportsman.

The United States Atlantic Tuna Tournament expressed their loss by instituting a Harry Peters Memorial Trophy awarded annually at the tournament.

Serious bluefin tuna anglers time their fishing so that it coincides perfectly with the migrations of these giant fish as they move North from the Caribbean. Two famed spots situated right in the path of this Northward migration are the tiny Bahama islands of Cat Cay and Bimini, and from the middle of May until the second week in June, schools of fish pass here almost daily. At this time, tuna anglers swarm to the islands where they engage in a series of tuna tournaments to pit their skills and muscle against the fish and against each other.

The Bahama International Tournament at Cat Cay, The Bimini Tournament and other tournaments here attract the best big-game anglers in the world, and the competition is so stiff that one mistake means a lost tournament. These anglers are here to catch fish, they have the equipment and the know how and everything about the tournaments are geared to one thing—taking the giant bluefins. The boats are the fastest and best in the world with virtually all of them equipped with tuna towers and triple controls so that the fish can be spotted while the captain steers from the most advantageous place—perched 20 feet above the water on the tower. The tackle is meant for big fish with 130 Pound Class Tycoon rods and 15/0 Fin-Nor reels loaded with 39 thread linen or dacron line. Then the new science of fighting big fish is demonstrated time after time in the tournaments for 500 pound fish may be boated in as little as 10 minutes from hookup.

Harry Peters is one of the best of these tournament anglers. A quick look around his office at W. H. Peters Inc., Cadillac distributor in Hackensack, N.J., shows more trophies than most anglers catch fish in a single season. He has a trophy from The New York Athletic Club for the biggest tuna taken during a year. He won all the marbles at Bimini one year and he won the biggest of all big game tournaments, The United States Atlantic Tuna Tournament. These plus countless others are among his personal victories and victories of teams he fished for.

The Bahama International Tournament is a contest of the best that is limited to 3 member teams from Canada, Bermuda, The Bahamas, Mexico, South Africa, Venezuela, Argentina, Puerto Rico and the United States. Harry Peters fishes for the U.S. team that is composed of 3 selected anglers whose background for fishing giant tuna makes them eligible for this team.

A typical day of tournament fishing for Harry Peters would begin at approximately 7 A.M. with breakfast. At Cat Cay it then means hopping on one of the station wagons that continually circle the island to get to the boats where he will discuss last minute strategy with his 3 teammates and the captains. All the anglers will be watching the weather closely as this is a primary factor determining if any fish will be caught that day. A perfect day at Cat Cay has a stiff Southwest wind that is really kicking up the water. A perfectly calm day is as bad for fishing as a day that is too rough to go out, for on each of these days the catches will be zero.

The crews of the tournament boats are all specialists in this fishing and every one of them is thoroughly efficient at his job. Harry Peters' crew consists of Captain Solano, first mate Al Ellison and second mate Carol Chance. These men have fished together for years and they execute their difficult jobs as smoothly as major league infielders. Harry Peters minces no words about the importance of a good crew for he says, "An angler is only 40% of taking a big fish while the boat is 60%."

His crew, as always, has all the technical aspects of the days fishing in go position for the 8 A.M. starting time. The bait will be aboard—mullet flown in from Florida which is now gutted and has the big 12/0 Sobey hooks sewn into the cavities. They will have lead weights painstakingly sewn into them so that the mullet will swim upright in the water. The bait and hook are attached to 15 feet of cable leader which is neatly coiled so that it can be snapped into the line on a moments notice. There will be four of these baits ready and in the freezer where they will stay until the tuna are actually sighted for in the Bahamas no bait goes over the side until the tuna are directly behind the boat.

A fisherman will go over his tackle lifting the Tycoon rod that is as thick as a baseball bat. This rod has strength enough to hold a team of horses, but before the day is out every ounce of that strength will be tested. The line will be checked making sure that there is only 30 feet of double line as more than 30 feet disqualifies an angler for strict International Game Fish Association Rules are adhered to in the tournaments. Harry Peters will check his line for any frayed sections in the line which would test out to having strength enough when wet to hold up 130 pounds of dead weight. Several frays could reduce its strength by 10 or 20 pounds and this could mean a parted line on a fish that should be caught. Then too he will check to see that the reel is packed evenly and tightly for when tuna run, the line must flow from the reel smoothly so that it doesn't jump and suddenly pop.

Eight o'clock and the big show is on the road as the boats race for the tuna grounds. The fleet of sleek fishing yachts racing at full throttle makes an almost poetic sight in the tropical water. It is exciting to see the captains sitting up in the towers controlling the boats as they bounce through the water and begin searching the schools of fish. Although the boats fan out over the area it will be the fastest and most maneuverable ones that will come to the school of fish first. Of the starting 40 to 50 boats in this contest approximately 10 to 12 of them will be Rybovich fishermen for it is a well known fact in Cat Cay, if you are going to bet on a winner of a tuna tournament pick a man with a Rybovich.

A 41 foot Rybovich fisherman powered by 2 Chrysler 275 horse power motors literally flies Harry Peters' boat through the water. This is his second Rybovich and he says, "I kept my first Rybovich 5 years and before that the longest I ever kept a boat was 18 months." These yachts are exclusively built for tournament sportsfishing as they are designed to be fast and highly maneuverable. They sit low in the water and one of their trademarks is the wide transom door that makes landing a big fish easier. Mr. Peters' boat has his main deck controls on the starboard side as he is in the habit of landing his fish on that side—each Rybovich is custom built to the anglers specifications."

This tournament angler cannot heap enough praise on the Rybovich fisherman and there no doubt would be more of them in the tournament except for the fact that the West Palm Beach, Florida, boatbuilder will make only 4 or 5 boats annually. If the reader wanted one he could call up Johnny Rybovich and send in a deposit to confirm his order which they would be very happy to take. The only drawback is that the wait for the boat will be from 2 to 3 years—so great is the demand for them. Their cost varies from a rock bottom price of $45,000 up to $150,000. An average Rybovich sportsfisherman with a flying bridge, a tuna tower, triple controls and a Rybovich fighting chair costs $60,000 to $90,000 depending on the size and amount of extra electrical equipment added.

Tuna Alley is the sky blue shallow water that stretches several miles offshore from the islands. This is where the boats hunt the migrating tuna schools looking for the fish as they swim only 2 or 3 feet under the surface. To the hunters the fish appear as dark blue sticks moving North in the water. Once a school is sighted the boat really pours it on for it will race almost head on toward the school of fish which may number 5 to 25 tuna and represent as much as 15,000 pounds of charging live tuna.

When the on rushing boat gets approximately 150 yards from the fish the captain will suddenly U-turn the boat and begin leading the school of fish. Now the boat slows up for the fish will be moving 8 to 10 miles an hour zig-zagging back and forth just under the surface of the water. These wild fish move about in no predictable manner and they give the anglers the same exciting feeling the old whalers had when they saw the big whales spouting.

A typical catch aboard Harry Peters' boat begins the moment Captain Solano first sights the fish. Everyone quickly takes battle positions. The mate snaps the cable and mullet bait to the line. Fisherman Peters takes to the fighting chair, placing the rod butt into the gimbal and fastening the hooks of his kidney harness to the reel. He is ready.

They hope the boat won't spook the fish as it might on a calm day, but the breeze is chopping up the surface keeping the boat out of the line of vision of the fish. As the boat turns and begins moving with the fish the angler lets his line and bait drop back 75 to 100 yards so that the mullet will be swimming right among the tuna. From the moment the bait had entered the water the angler is completely on his own for now no one may touch the rod or line while he is fishing. This is a firm rule of The International Game Fish Association and it holds even if the fish were to knock an angler out of the boat. This has happened and Harry Peters laughingly says, "I almost got knocked overboard on a couple of occasions myself, but somehow I managed to catch myself."

The tuna will move on one side of the bait first, and then on the other side, occasionally, dipping under it. The angler jigs the bait moving his rod tip up and letting it down; he drops back a little line and reels some line in. If they still don't hit the captain may speed the boat up slightly and then slow up trying to induce a hit. Finally one comes over and wacks the mullet. Now the angler rears back pulling the rod back once, twice, three times to hook his fish.

Once the hook is set and the fish knows he is in trouble, he boils splashing water in all directions. Then he takes off on a wild frenzied run racing as fast as his giant streamlined body will take him. The angler must immediately drop his rod tip and lower the drag down to less than 10 pounds of holding pressure. This is the fish's round for he is completely fresh and gamey and he has one of the strongest bodies of any living thing working for him. He breaks out of the school streaking through the water 100, 200, 300, 1,000 or 2,000 yards at a speed estimated to be up to 45 miles an hour. There is nothing the angler can do but to drop the rod tip and watch line race off his big reel.

The second the fish is on, everyone's work is geared to bring this 500 pound fish in immediately. The captain stays at the control and watches the fish while he races the boat forward to parallel the run of the fish. One mate gets behind Mr. Peters and his job is to constantly point the chair in the direction of the fish as the rod must never bend sideways for this snaps lines and breaks guides. Second mate Carol Chance raises the red flag which tells the other boats—Fish on! Get the hell out of our way!

The action is electric as the boat races parallel to the running fish. A big U-bend or belly develops in the line and the angler immediately has his job cut out for him—get that belly out of the line and get a straight tight line to the fish. The sooner the better for when the fish stops running if he has slack line he has a better than even chance of spitting the hook. Now the angler cranks and cranks and cranks. This is tiring work and even with the 3 to 1 gear ratio it feels like you reel forever to bring in that ¼ of a mile of line.

Finally, after what seemed like an eternity a direct line is made between the angler and his fish. Then the basic maneuver of all big-game angling—the torturous pumping of the rod back and forth to reel in the precious few feet of line is begun. It takes all the power in a man's arms and body to lift that rod tip up. Then there is that estatic second of relief while the rod tip is dropped and ever so little line is gained. Immediately the second pull back and lift of the rod tip is begun followed by the drop. Again and again and again the torture of the pull is upon the angler until every one of his muscles are numb. Philip Wylie so deftly termed this as time in the torture chair.

Harry Peters has prepared for this fishing well in advance with workouts in gyms and at home. He now uses all the muscles in his body plus all the skill he gained from hundreds of hours of fighting. He works his fish hard and business-like, never giving the fish a moment's respite for he says, "When you're tournament fishing you're out there to bring the fish in and score points. You're here to win, so the faster the fish comes in the better the chance for hunting another school and taking a second fish." At Cat Cay there exists another reason for rushing a tuna and that is sharks. Mr. Peters says blandly, "A tuna must be taken within ½ hour or they are sure to be sharked."

Tuna are bleeders therefore they are the worst kind of fish to have on the line in shark waters as sharks can smell blood diluted to 1 drop of blood to 1,000,000 drops of water. The bleeding fish quickly attract them. In tournament fishing sharks add tension, for any fish so much as touched by a shark is disqualified for tournament points and no angler wants his fish disqualified.

There is a sharp drop off at Cat Cay that runs all along the area several miles off shore. Here the water abruptly drops down into the deep tropical ocean and it is near this ledge that the heaviest shark concentrations are found. Many anglers feel that fish that reach the drop off might as well be cut off the line as they are almost certain to be mutilated. Then too, it takes three times as long to get a fish in deep water than it does in shallow water so all efforts must constantly be made to keep the fish away from the drop. The anglers will take chances by upping the drag when a fish gets near the drop. Skilled captains can greatly aid an angler, for a good captain keeps the boat between the drop and the fish and herds the tuna away from there. Sometimes a captain may close in on a fish to scare it into running toward safe water.

The tournament anglers and captains know this sport and they work together as well knit teams to beat these giant fish that weigh from 400 to 600 pounds. A captain must do everything possible to aid the angler. One important task is to constantly keep the boat and fish in position. The perfect position is to have the fish directly behind the boat and facing the boat. The fish are seldom cooperative for they tend to run sideways away from a boat therefore there is constant maneuvering of the boat. When the fish is directly behind the boat the captain can throw the boat in reverse, thus giving the angler a chance to reel line in quickly and get in tight to his fish.

As the fight progresses, the tuna will begin to tire and his runs will shorten. He may be worked in as close as 50 yards from the boat. The fish may even act tired but the angler must never let up on the pressure for this can give the fish his second wind. The angler must continue to lean back and pump with his own last ounce of energy to get that fish in the remaining distance.

Often the fish will refuse to cooperate and will run stripping the line the angler has worked so hard to capture. Then there is only one thing to do, drop the rod tip and let the fish run. After the run, which will not be as long or hard as the first runs, it is back to work—reset the drag at 20 to 30 pounds and pull the rod until the tip points towards heaven and then drop it while a few precious feet of line is reeled in. This is done 5, 10, 15, 20 or 100 times more and then the fish may only be 40 yards off the stern. There is more work ahead and there is no time to slack off now, for that fish must be lead in. The radio will crackle that one boat already has theirs—then another one. The angler knows if he is to stay in the running this fish is a must.

Finally the happy sight everybody waited for and the double line breaks over the back for the first time. This means there is just 30 feet of line left out there and quickly the angler changes tactics. He reaches up with his gloved left hand and begins hand lining the remaining line on the rod while his right hand continues cranking the reel. Behind the 30 feet of double line is the 15 feet of cable and when that comes over the mate looses no time in grabbing this leader. This is the first time the angler is permitted assistance and it's a relief to have the mate take over. Still everyone aboard knows this fish isn't through—not a tuna—as the fish is more confused and dazed than he is worn out.

Anglers know the most important thing for them to do during a landing is to drop the drag pressure to less than 10 pounds. The fish is still green and if he suddenly reconsiders he would pop a tight line like a spider web. In these close quarters the low drag pressure gives the fish practically a free line and it avoids breaks.

The tuna may be splashing around for often it is difficult to get the gaff in him. Suddenly he may decide to run and he will rip the leader from the mates hand effortlessly and take line with him. He is out there and the angler must go back to work to bring him in again.

Suddenly there may be a dorsal fin sighted or several dark shapes may be seen in the water. Sharks! They begin circling the fish and the angler knows it is only a matter of minutes before one closes for a kill which would rip 20 or 30 pounds of flesh from the fish. This will mean all this hard work is for nothing as an injured fish won't score a single point. Here the anglers have their choice. Some will quickly break out a shark repellant which they attach to the line and let it slide down to the fish. The repellent discolors the water into a squidlike ink thus frightening the sharks away. There exists a sharp difference of opinion as to the value of the repellents and Harry Peters for one does not use them as he feels they do not keep the sharks away. "Worse yet," he says, "they scare the life out of the tuna and cause the fish to go crazy on the line." He feels the only way to beat the sharks is to bring the fish in fast before they can attack. If an angler feels a dull thud on his line he knows he has had it for this is the tell tale feeling one gets when a shark rips a 30 pound piece of meat from his quarry.

Most tournament anglers agree that when sharks are about the best thing to do is to bring a fish in as fast as the angler's muscles, tackle and skill will let him. At this time the angler really has to rear back and get more pull than ever before into the rod. He pulls until he thinks his arms will rip out of their sockets and he pulls until he feels the harness will cut his body in half. Get the rod up, drop it, and reel in a little, again and again and again, just as fast as possible. Once the sharks are there they do not go away but continue circling and watching. If the angler is lucky that double line and cable will again reappear before an attack. The mate again grabs the leader while the other mate is ready with the ten foot handle of the flying gaff. There will be urgency in their work for sharks have been known to come right up and hit a fish even as it is being boated.

The mate waits for the right second and then he brings the long handle of the flying gaff up sinking the big hook deep into the fleshy section of the tuna. The handle of the flying gaff breaks off leaving the tuna securely held by the gaff hook and the stout line running from it. The transom of the Rybovich sportsman is swung open and the bloody furiously kicking 500 pound tuna is hauled in. The fish is angry and scared as it bounces around frantically. Quickly a mate grabs a baseball bat-like club and with all his might smashes at the skull of the fish 5 to 10 times to quiet him.

The fish flips feebly as the fight is over and only the cleanup remains. The first thing is to plug up the hole in the body of the fish where the gaff had been sunk. It is still leaking blood all over the deck. One mate stuffs rags into the hole to stop the flow of blood while the other mate hoses the deck cleaning the blood and slime away. It has been 25 minutes since hookup when the captain radios they have boated their tuna and it goes at least 500 pounds. Everyone will be quite sure the shark never touched the fish, but still they inspect it to confirm the fact. Not a mark on the tuna and there lay 500 glorious points. Already a half a dozen other boats have boated fish so that it only stands to reason some of these may be a little bigger and will give that angler a lead of a few points.

Quickly everyone fades back to their hunting stations—the captain gets back up on the tower and begins searching tuna alley for fish again. Every angler knows a double will really put him out there ahead of the pack. Harry Peters remembers the day in 1962 when in the morning they hit a big one. That fight, even from a perfectionist point of view, was almost perfect for in exactly 12 minutes they boated a 577 pounder. A little later they sighted another school and a second fish hit their trailing mullet. The second one seemed even bigger but the angler had the know how, the equipment and he was in top physical condition, so 20 minutes later a 587 pounder was hauled through the transom door. That feat amounted to boating 1,164 pounds of tuna in 32 minutes of fighting—that is fishing. This double was instrumental in Mr. Peters taking the big trophy at Bimini that year.

The tournament anglers will search the fish all day long and three o'clock comes all to soon for them. Unless an angler is fighting a fish this means all throttle back to the official weighing station. There may be as many as twenty or thirty tuna awaiting official inspection and weights so that the angler will have a wait of several hours before his official score is posted. It is a good feeling to have a fish and know that you are up there with the leaders.

When tuna are taken in the Bahamas they will have practically nothing in their stomachs. The stomach will be the size and shape of a football bladder, yet inside there will be less food substance than can fit on the palm of an outstretched hand. This leads to the theory that the fish were completely off feed in the warm Caribbean breeding grounds and only now while on the move North will they begin to eat. Some insist that during the fight the fish regurgitate any food substance that is in their stomach, but this does not seem probable in view of the record speed these fish have been brought in. Another reason would be that it does not happen with other specie of fish nor does it happen when the fish are up North and are feeding.

After the fish are inspected, weighed and the official scores are posted on the bulletin board each angler will know exactly what he has to do the next day. There will be two more days of pressure fishing and tenseness will build up among those anglers who have a chance to win. To these anglers the second day is even more important than the first, for the other angler's lead must be cut or you must protect your own lead. Then too there always exists the possibility that the third day will be a bad one where weather stops fishing or worse where the whole fleet might go out and take no fish. Every angler knows that the second day leader then takes the trophy.

Most of the time there is a final day that usually shapes up as a tense battle between the leaders. There may be 5 or 6 boats all in contention at this showdown. Everyone at sea and on land will follow the action by short wave radio. The radio may suddenly crackle that Harry Peters has one on, or another angler boated a fish, however there may be a 300 pound variance between fish so that the final outcome will not be known until the weigh in. One tournament angler once had the trophy won until the judges discovered that accidentally he had been fishing with 31 feet of double line and he was disqualified.

When the big trophy is finally awarded the angler who wins will be proud, yet receiving the trophy itself may be somewhat of a letdown since the real thrill was fighting the fish and winning. This is true of most sportsmen whether track stars, fishermen or even professional baseball players who may make 100% of a year's salary for a world series share all admit the real thrill is the winning.

One point of the tournament anglers is that they are sportsmen and many of them, like Harry Peters, are quite proud of the fact that the fish they catch are never wasted. Their catches today are aiding science in many ways. When ichthyologists want to study a certain specie of gamefish, they generally contact the tournament director and make arrangements to collect all the fish they need for their study. One point recently discovered was that a tuna's eye has a retina very similar to a human eye and the intriguing possibility of fish to man retina transplants may be a thing of the future. The carcass of the fish at Bimini and Cat Cay will go to feed the fish of the Michael Lerner Aquarium or they will feed the sharks that are kept in tanks on the island. Scientists here are continually studying sharks to see if they can learn ways to stop shark attacks on humans and our Navy is very much interested in this work. The fish taken in the U.S. Atlantic Tuna Tournament at Rhode Island are sold to local canneries and the money from the sales is divided up among three charities.

During 1961, many of the catches of the May run at Cat Cay were tagged and released by these anglers. All told 5 of the released fish were later recaptured off Bergen Norway some 5,000 miles distant. One of these fish had been recaptured only 118 days after tagging meaning it traveled almost 50 miles a day, gaining weight while it did so. These captures were more than merely interesting as they definitely disproved an old theory about tuna migrations that claimed the North American tuna did not cross the Atlantic to Europe and that the European tuna did not come to North America. Now it seems more likely that there is a somewhat circular migration of the fish with them coming out of the Caribbean in the spring and moving North to New England, Nova Scotia or to the European waters. When cold weather sets in, the fish return to their wintering grounds in the Caribbean. More tagging experiments will either prove, modify or completely disprove this theory, but one thing is certain the fish used for tagging will definitely come from these sportsmen.

After the giant tuna pass the Cat Cay area, they keep moving North. No one knows the exact route they take as there are no other fishing grounds between the Bahamas and the New Jersey-New England area. It is generally believed the fish more or less follow the Gulf Stream North to these feeding grounds. It is interesting to note that the smaller bluefins, often referred to as school tuna, spread themselves over almost the whole coast line where they stay offshore while the giant tuna will come into their favorite spots that are relatively close to shore. They come to the same areas year after year.

Recently there was a dropoff of fish coming into Nova Scotia. Such famous spots as Soldier's Rip was barren of tuna. Even the big Nova Scotia International Tuna Tournament had to be cancelled for a number of years because of the lack of fish. I asked Mr. Peters what his theory was of why this spot, where the biggest tuna in the world including Commodore Hodgson's world record 977 pounder, had dried up? His answer was obvious and clear, "No bait. When there is no bait in these Northern waters the fish simply move to another area where they find bait."

Beginning in August, the same general group of tuna anglers that had fished Cat Cay will begin to congregate at Montauk Point, New York, or Galilee, Rhode Island, to try for the tuna that come into these waters. Hundreds of other anglers from the metropolitan Northeast join in the fun that amounts to one of the biggest fish hunts anywhere in the world.

The fish taken here will average 100 pounds more than they did at Cat Cay as they will be constantly feeding. The method of fishing here invites more anglers to join in as fast boats are not essential to take the fish, since most fish will be hooked from a stationary boat. Here the anglers build up a chum line and then slip a baited hook out in the line as the tuna begin feeding.

One of the big events in the Northeast is the United States

Atlantic Tuna Tournament which is run in September and is based in Galilee, Rhode Island. This is the biggest big-game fishing tournament in the world and is currently attracting more than 500 anglers and 150 boats. Harry Peters was the President of the tournament, for several years, but unlike former presidents he is also a past winner of the event. The story of his 1959 victory for himself and the Montauk Yacht Club that he then fished for is an interesting one. He took the tournament in an extremely bad tuna year for no fish had been taken in the area right up to tournament time and there were even some thoughts of canceling it.

A few days before tournament time he was out fishing in the waters North of Montauk Point. Quite by accident, the radio was on and the conversation between two commercial draggers was overheard. One warned the other to keep away from a hole on Cox's Ledge as there were tuna down there. This is quite common as big tuna can rip nets to shreds and commercial fishermen of the area have a traditional hatred for the fish that dates back to the days before the tuna meat was commercially marketable and the fish merely tore up nets.

None of them had ever heard of the hole before so they took out their charts and fisherman, captain and crew pored over them to locate the spot. Then sure enough, in an area near Cox's Ledge there appeared two distinct dropoffs where the water dropped to 24 and 36 fathoms. They knew this must be the hole. Harry Peters took mind of the incident and the next evening when the board of Governors of the tournament met to go over the last minute rules Mr. Peters suggested they broaden the bounderies for fishing that year as he had heard there were tuna in the area known as "the hole." They were quite willing to accept the recommendation as any news of tuna was good news that year.

On tournament day, he headed straight for the hole. First he chose the deeper of the two depressions and using a small spinning rod he lowered a baited hook down to pick up some whiting. There were no hits and that meant that there would be no tuna in that hole. Quickly they moved to the other hole and again the spinning line was lowered and within a few moments a whiting came up, then another and another—the hole was filled with them, therefore, if there were tuna in the area they would be here.

Quickly, mate Al Ellison baited up the whiting and it went down. Harry Peters started jigging it when suddenly his big rod bent in half as a fish struck the bait. He missed it but they were all encouraged by the miss for it proved there were big fish here. They had the hole all to themselves as no other boat chose to fish here and they felt confident they would hook the next one.

Half an hour later they had their second hit and this time the fish stayed on. There still remained the distinct possibility that their tuna could turn out to be a shark as this fishing is done deep and an angler can never be certain of just what strikes his line until he surfaces the fish. According to tournament rules, the captain radioed that they had a fish on while the angler slugged it out. It is much harder to fight a tuna in deep water for when they are down it is a back breaking job to bring them up. Still within a half an hour they boated the fish—it was a tuna alright, a 465 pounder. The captain again radioed they had boated their fish and they went on and tried for a double, but they didn't get another strike the rest of the day. In fact, it was a trying day in the whole flotilla, for that was the only tuna taken that day or any other day of the three day tournament. That fish won the tournament!

This is highly competitive fishing and some anglers were a little hot over the capture. All kinds of accusations were made including that they had fished out of bounds, that they had failed to radio in, and even that they had the fish hidden on board before the tournament started. All these accusations were of course, ridiculous, for through smart and alert fishing they had won the biggest of all tuna tournaments in a year when all the other anglers failed to score.

Just how hard a big tuna is to capture may best be illustrated by the fish Mr. Peters once hooked off Block Island. "From the moment he was on I knew I had an exceptionally big fish and I knew we were going to have a fight," he said. And what a battle they had for it stretched from one hour to the next with neither fisherman nor fish giving an inch. This fish was all power and during the fight it actually dragged the boat against its motors a distance of 10 miles. It was pump and reel, pump and reel, pump and reel, all day long with the fish never seeming to tire. Three times the fish was at the side of the boat, but they couldn't bring him in as he was far too green to gaff. Each time he broke away and it meant more work.

Eight hours later it was getting dark and both angler and fish were in a completely exhausted state. The fish suddenly turned and the line went slack and the biggest fish Harry Peters ever had in all his years of fishing simply dropped off the hook. The crew and the angler agreed this fish may well have exceeded 1,000 pounds, for none had ever seen one that rivaled it in size and strength.

This prize was lost because in the course of a particularly hard fight a hook will begin to wear a groove in the fishes mouth. As the fight continues the hook keeps working back and forth and this groove gets bigger all the time until it makes a hole big enough for the hook to slip out of when a fish turns. This is exactly what happened here.

I asked him how he felt after hours of fighting a fish. His answer was surprising. "Mad!" He said, "I get mad at my inability to bring a fish in and it makes me work harder and get still madder." Another fish took him over 4½ hours to capture and this one weighed just over 600 pounds. Fighting tuna is strange for his biggest capture a 772 pound wopper took exactly 20 minutes to boat. What happened was the leader wrapped around the tail of the fish and in this way rendered the bluefin almost helpless, therefore in spite of its size and strength it was relatively easy to bring in.

Harry Peters loves catching big fish and he is one of the expert deep-sea anglers of the country. Probably his best love is tuna tournament fishing because of the extra measure of competition added to this already tremendously challenging sport. The three most important tournaments are the Bahama International Tournament, The U.S. Atlantic Tuna Tournament and the Nova Scotia International Tournament. Today, with the Nova Scotia Tournament in mothballs, the Bimini Tournament replaces this as number three on the roster of the big three tournaments. As soon as Mr. Peters adds the Bahama Tournament to his string of victories he will have all three in the bag—a feat unequalled in tournament fishing.

It is more valid, perhaps, to judge what kind of a sportsman a man is by considering his reaction to losing a fish rather than to his catching one. In tournament fishing it is particularly difficult for most men to keep everything in its proper perspective when faced with the possible disqualification of a sizable fish that would unquestionably prove a factor in deciding the outcome of the contest. Four such disqualifications in recent years come to mind. Two of these resulted in heated and protracted arguments during which the integrity of the judges and officials was questioned, while a third saw an angler break down and cry when his only chance of winning was removed. The fourth one involved Harry Peters.

About ten years ago, with his team a strong contender in the United States Atlantic Tuna Tournament, Harry hooked a large tuna only to have the leader part. The line was reeled in, a new leader hastily measured off and attached by one of the crew, and the fish eventually rehooked and boated. The fish weighed almost four hundred pounds when it was put up on the rack at dockside. Then it was announced that the fish would probably have to be disqualified because the tackle judges had discovered that the leader used was slightly over the fifteen foot maximum length allowed. Harry walked over to the judges, examined the leader himself, and slowly shook his head. "I guess that's it then," he said quietly. "That's the way it goes sometimes." Then he smiled and walked back to his boat, *Lazy Bones*. No fury, no outward display of inward disappointment and frustration, no recriminations against the crew for the mistake or against the judges for the technicality. Disqualified by a minor infraction, which probably gave him no real advantage to begin with, he had accepted the judgment in a gentlemanly manner that those who knew him had come to expect. There would be other days for him before he died a few years later—but not that particular day.

Sportsmanship is a quality more easily recognized than defined. For the crowd that pressed around the weigh-in stand near sunset in Point Judith on that cool summer evening some ten years ago, no definition was necessary. They had seen it, and, for many of them, that disqualified fish had far more meaning than the hundreds of others that Harry Peters ever caught.

Edward Bartley
Director
United States Atlantic Tuna Tournament

INDEX